FEARLESS REFERRALS

Ask in a Way that is Comfortable for YOU and Market Yourself for Free

MATT ANDERSON

ISBN: 1-4392-6481-3
ISBN-13: 9781439264812

To Mum

Table of Contents

Acknowledgements

For about three years I wanted to write a book but didn't believe I belonged on the same shelves as the authors I admired. Then I did start writing this book (well over two years ago) but got frustrated trying to make the time for it when I needed to be earning money and paying bills. I was not convinced it would make a difference for anyone.

I would not have completed this book for I-don't-know-how-long had it not been because of a project I committed to in Landmark Education's Self Expression and Leadership course. Thank you, Wayne Fettman, for your belief in me. The support of the people in this class and me making the verbal commitment to them made all the difference in putting the leverage I needed for myself to follow through. I now understand why so many people have shared with me over the years "Oh yeah, I want to write a book too. I just need to find the time!" It is not easy! And I didn't have a family to support so I can empathize with any aspiring writer.

But this book did need writing as referrals are what every business owner, sales person and professional responsible for generating business likes best. They are the ultimate compliment that says you have done a good job and another person is endorsing you.

I have now spent over seven years helping people bring in more referral business and the results I get with my coaching clients now create the urgency for me to get this information out to you so you can reap the rewards as well.

I am grateful to many inspiring business and personal development minds without whom I would never have survived in business to put me back on track on the rough days. Stephen Covey and Brian Tracy are the two most prominent but the reinforcement I got from everyone listed on my bibliography only proves to me that we all need frequent support from many sources. Thank you to you all: your writing made a difference.

My own networking experiences and endless cups of coffee (and beers) have taken me all over not only the US but the UK, even parts of Canada. I have learned from at least seven chamber of commerce memberships, leadership training in England and the US with Business Network International, NAIFA's LILI program, multiple other leads groups, dozens of other networking events, hundreds of seminars and workshops with a wide variety of professions, serving on boards, committees and even my share of network marketing events.

But my best referral learning has come from doing it myself first and then coaching others how to get the same results. I have learned from the great successes to those who could not get off square one – and everyone in between. Never a dull moment! Thank you to all those who have trusted me with their hard-earned income.

While I cannot mention everyone who deserves the thanks for helping me along the way, a final special thank you:

-to Mum for your support long before anyone else thought I would make it. Thank you for your patience. I have finally learned how powerful it is to be supported. You have been telling me since I was little that I would go places and make an impact on the world. You have no idea how important those words of encouragement have meant.

- to the happy memory of my father, Pop. I know you're still around waiting to pick me up from somewhere or other.

-to my assistant, Susie Switzer-Krohn, who has been a rock in taking care of all the details I miss in my business. I know I do not take enough time to let you know how much I appreciate all you do. Hopefully something permanent here will help a little!

-to my editor Angie Finch for putting so much into doing outstanding work on this book. It was a pleasure working with you and so easy. Sorry we couldn't meet when I spoke in Atlantic City a while ago. I hope anyone interested in working with 'the best' contacts you at ahfinch@optonline.net – I could not recommend anyone more highly!

- to Kirk Anderson (no relation) for the hilarious cartoons. I am so glad we have rekindled an old friendship that started at Briarpatch in '91. You are brilliantly talented and really should be famous. Thanks for letting me stay over at your place even if I won't eat your Marmite from 1964. Again, I hope people see this work and are knocking down your door: kirka@infionline.net

- to my uncle, Richard Yeomans, for producing the cover. I was delighted when you agreed to do this and for bringing more family into this. Thank you again! Oh, about that second book…

- to Mark Mantell and John Gray at New York Life for believing in my work earlier than any other company on a national level. It was terrific fun coming to New York to record the training videos. I will never forget those opportunities. Although I can't understand why you didn't like the Cheesehead! None of this would have happened without Eric Heiting who made the first introduction. Thanks, Eric!

- to Scott Downs at MetLife for believing in my work and committing to results over the long haul. It has been a great experience and I truly appreciate the faith you have in me.

- to Juli McNeely, Mike Smith, Susan Linck, Liz Pollock and everyone at NAIFA-Wisconsin for accepting me as an outsider and allowing me to get involved and be part of a great association

- to Sean Bailey at Horsesmouth.com for taking me on as a contributing author in 2007 and publishing my writing ever since. This boosted my confidence that I belonged on a national stage.

- to Hugh Mason for your friendship and for opening the first doors for me in the UK. Who would have thought that the 5th Concerto and *The Young Adult* would take us here?!

-to Steve Garrison for inspiring me to get the book completed. You sharing about how you were doing the same has pushed me on the days I thought I should do something else with my time. Good luck with your bestseller: *The Five Secrets From Oz*!

Preface

I am writing this book because I want you to know that you can grow a business successfully through referrals—and you already know how rewarding that can be, otherwise you would not have picked this book up. It is not easy, and I want you to know that right up front, too. I am not going to fill your head with false hype that you will have referrals coming out of your ears after Chapter 1. I know we all want something that's easy, but getting to that point will take most of you some time to accomplish. You can get referrals easily too—once you have the skill set.

And this is what really excites me so much: there IS a way to grow your business by word-of-mouth. You have it in your hands. And you don't need to be great-looking or have the gift of the gab to do it. You do not have to be a natural at building spectacular relationships or have the personality of a Santa Claus. You don't even need a dynamic sense of humor or white teeth or a full head of hair.

What is in this book WORKS. And it will work for you if you follow what I suggest. And if it doesn't work, it is partly because of the challenge.

Here is the challenge: many people who start their own business or go into sales do so because they like the independence. That's great—however, you don't need to reinvent every wheel because you see yourself as a do-it-yourselfer. I speak from painful experience of someone who tried for many years! Simply follow what is recommended in this book and you will get faster results. I promise.

I also want you to know that I have made all the same mistakes everyone else has on my journey to learning what I will share in this book. I am a fairly introverted and shy Englishman living in the USA. I used to be a conservative no-risk-taking elementary and middle school teacher who liked his steady paycheck and benefits.

But I was also one of those people who was always thinking of business ideas and then letting that voice in my head instantly talk me out of it. That I should stick to my safe place and put up with being surrounded by a majority of peers (not all) who could not wait for Friday to come along. Yet I felt a bit of a failure in front of the children sometimes—that my life experience was from studying but not really from much doing. I had this increasing sense that I was not living life or fulfilling my potential.

Well I finally got so unhappy as a teacher, working too many hours and feeling burned out on people, that I left the profession and stumbled around for two years not quite sure what to do next. Then a former girlfriend from Russia got back in touch and, not having any better ideas, I thought I might get a teaching certificate so I could go there and work. This was a foolproof idea until about a week later when I realized I was tired of teaching, I had not enjoyed being in Moscow when I had visited, and I really was not in love with this woman!

I will never forget how miserable I was that March lunchtime lying on my stomach on the same bed my father had spent his last months when he was dying from cancer at 58. I was completely stuck and thoroughly down in the dumps.

The one habit that saved me was buying personal development books. That afternoon my mother and I went to Leamington Spa and on the upstairs floor of Waterstones I picked a book off a shelf called *Be Your Own Life Coach* by Fiona Harrold. I had no idea what a life coach was, but her book felt like an IV of both adrenaline and inspiration for me. She talked about confidence and starting your own business and taking responsibility for your life. She had me clean up my past and start believing in myself and believing that what I wanted was possible.

Perhaps for the first time since things my mother said to me during childhood, I began to say to myself: "Maybe I can do it." It was exactly what I needed and it gave me the burst of self-esteem to get back on a plane to the USA, move to a completely new area (the mountains of New Mexico) and start my first business enterprises (which both "failed" by the way but that's for another story!).

I started on square minus one, quite frankly. Other than a grandfather who ran many different business enterprises before I knew him, including a fish and chip shop, but who ended up a vacuum cleaner salesman in his 60's (that seemed to be more the butt of jokes), there were no business role models in my family. Everybody was an educator of some kind.

I moved to Albuquerque in 2002, which was exciting and quite foolish. Little did I know that New Mexico was the third poorest state in the union at the time. Little did I know that when you are starting a business, it helps to know people! I knew nobody in a city of 750,000. So I networked like a madman. I joined two business leads groups, a gym, a chamber of commerce and a Toastmasters chapter. I read as many books as I could get my hands on and started a second business!

And everywhere I went I asked people where they got their business. What struck me was how almost everyone I asked would say "word of mouth." I was hoping they would mention specific places I could go too to get business but it was always this idea that other people spoke highly of them and opened doors to new business. Nobody ever said: "Oh, it was this ingenius direct mail campaign I did" or "Radio advertising"—I suppose they wouldn't have been networking if that were true.

So I was intrigued. But what I quickly found out was that most professionals from all walks of life were talking about unsolicited referrals—ones they had not asked for—when they talked about "word-of-mouth." AND that this was not enough to live on! In addition, not only were most people not asking for referrals, but they didn't know what to say to get them! And a lot of people were not really doing anything to earn referrals either. They were just doing the same job everyone else in their industry was doing (they had just never stopped to notice or admit such a possibility).

I started talking to managers and trainers to find out what kind of help their salespeople were getting. This was interesting, too. A few had some kind of training system they had tried but it seldom stuck. Sometimes the manager had found a way to get referrals but their way didn't seem to work for their team. Mostly there was no training. Or the person at the top would say something unhelpful like; 'well all they need to do is ask!' as if the solution were always that simple. Maybe it worked in the 1970s.

I had stumbled onto something that was really important to sales people and yet hardly being addressed! For myself, I was so scared to cold call, but so liked the idea of running my own business that my mind raced (mostly out of desperation) to find ways to get more referrals just so I could stay in business. Because I networked so much, I started training groups how to network and get referrals—it didn't take that long to have something useful to share. That's the first time I learned about "the challenge."

I would present to a group a few ideas on what they could do to get more referrals, and then six weeks later I would return to cover a different topic. But invariably what I would find when I returned was that one or two people had made some changes in educating others how to refer them and that the remainder of the room consisted of a group of stubborn do-it-yourselfers who had ignored my suggestions so they could prove to themselves that they could figure it out for themselves—and usually fail.

But it's not all from being too independent. Some of the skill in getting referrals is counter-intuitive and some of it can feel a little labor-intensive. So, do you want results or the same old same old?

You know by now that getting referrals is not a quick fix or a software program.

If it was easy, everyone would get lots of referrals.

In a recent book titled, *Talent is Overrated*, author Geoff Colvin argues that high performers in every field **pursue DELIBERATE PRACTICE in areas that address specific skills that take them AROUND their limitations.**
This is what you need to do if you want more referral business. Getting good at referrals is no different: ***"If the activities that led to greatness were easy and fun, then everyone would do them, and they would not distinguish the best from the rest. The reality that deliberate practice is hard can even be seen as good news. It means that most people won't do it. So your willingness to do it will distinguish you all the more."***

This is what you need to do if you want more referral business—deliberate practice. And I'd like to commend you for taking the first step: proactively improving your referral skills by reading this book.

What Are Your Results Getting Referrals?

I recently conducted a seminar and asked the audience to share what they already know about getting referrals. Their list was long, including ideas such as: ask for referrals; provide good customer service; build trust; add value; build relationships; follow-up promptly; know your stuff; develop friendships; and use an agenda. (If my seminar were on how to get in great shape, I would have accumulated an equally impressive list.)

Next I asked the group for a show of hands of those who knew the rules of football. Many hands went into the air, so I asked whether we should all get together and scrimmage the nearest NFL team. I got some rather strange looks. The point is: Just because you know *how* to do something doesn't mean you have the commitment to follow-through, the stamina to do what is necessary, and the "stick-to-it-ness" that is required.

You're getting my point, right? Many of the people at this seminar were not there because they did not know many of the important factors that help us all get referrals. It's quite possible they *thought* they didn't know. But they did. So, what are the determining factors? It's likely that you too already know many of the important ways to get referrals, but are your results disappointing? What do you need to do differently? That's what this book is for.

Here are a few tips to get the most out of this book:

Schedule time to review what you've learned and practice it right away! If you are scheduling time to read professionally, you are already in a tiny percentage of the business world. Congratulations. Very few people continue to grow by going the extra inch on a daily basis (not mile – a more empowering mindset encouraged by Tony Allesandro). However, it's not what you know, it's what you do with what you know that counts.

1. **Take notes either on the inside cover pages of this book or somewhere you can revisit easily.** PLEASE, write all over the pages, highlight helpful passages. Make this a tool not a museum piece.
2. **Schedule the final few minutes of your reading time to consider ideas you want to implement.** If you have 30 minutes set aside for reading, use the last 5 minutes to review your notes or highlighted areas and decide how you're going to use these ideas.
3. **Revisit all of your notes on a regular basis and look for ways to take action.** Rather than launching into yet another book, go back through your notes on a monthly basis.
4. **Practice what sounds useful as soon as possible.** Action is the only way to improve your skills—and your results.

"Repetition is the mother of success."

—Tony Robbins

As you read this book, keep asking yourself: How can I implement this into my own business? Don't wait to start using what you learn here to get more referrals. It's never too early to put your radar out for happy clients who may be ready to refer you to others.

The sooner you start using these ideas, the sooner you can hone them to fit your personality. **You may need to hear an idea 10-30 times before the light goes on, sometimes more**. I think this point is not emphasized enough. Do you ever take action on a brand new idea the first time you hear it? It's very rare. Hearing an idea once seldom raises enough credibility in our minds for us to take action. Most of us need to hear something multiple times before we will ever do anything and the light bulb goes on.

Why do most high achievers recommend that you read their book multiple times? I'm embarrassed to admit I used to think it was because their egos were too big. "I'll decide if your ideas are any good; I don't need to do that," I said to myself. "I don't have time for that!" And then I'd hurry on to read something else and miss a lot of important ideas.

Certainly, we should question everything we hear and it does need to fit who we are, but virtually the oldest adage out there is **if you want to be successful, do what successful people do.** I recommend that you engrain this material by revisiting it regularly: You will get more referrals!

CHAPTER 1:

The Fearless Referral Fundamentals

> *"We are about to enter the age of word-of-mouth... even in this age of mass communication and multi-million dollar advertising campaigns, (it) is still the most important form of human communication."*
>
> —Malcolm Gladwell, *The Tipping Point*

1. 5-15-50-80

How exactly do I define a "referral"?

a) **A referral is when your referral source (Person A) recommends you to Person B because Person A is really pleased with the work you have done.**

In other words you are being recommended for all the right reasons because you have done a good job. There is nothing cheesy or borderline manipulative going on.

Not all referrals are created equally. One fact we have to acknowledge right away is that the quality of referrals can vary a lot! How enthusiastically people communicate about you and how strong the relationships are between you and Person A, and Person A and Person B make a huge difference.

The lowest quality referral is when you are given the name and number of Person B and he or she is not expecting your call. Because these referrals are so poor in quality in this day and age, this book is not going to spend time on clever techniques to generate a list of names. That is not an effective word-of-mouth endorsement.

b) **Person B should want to talk to you—or at least be open to hearing from you!**

You want to get your referral prospects warmed up so they that they actually want to hear from you! That's how to run a business that works, is fun, and is based on developing quality relationships.

Why is it so important to have a prospect expecting your call? What's wrong with just calling someone and name dropping with this unsuspecting person (apart from the fact you don't like it when it's done to you!)?

The Sandler Sales Institute studied this several years ago, and my experience over the years has found their numbers to be remarkably accurate. Here's how often the following turned into *business* (not just an appointment):

- **5%:** at best the amount of business you'll get from cold calls.

- **15%:** the amount of business you'll get when you use a name and say; "Sarah Megson gave me your name" – but your call is NOT expected. And that person may be a little puzzled why Sarah never mentioned anything to them. To the other person, it feels like a cold call. Many people get suspicious.

- **50%:** the amount of business you'll get **when you have permission to call and your call IS expected** and you say; "Sarah Megson suggested I call," and they reply, "Oh, yes, that's right. Yes, she did tell me about you."

  (By the way, **your next question is**: "Good. Actually I'm curious: what did Sarah share with you?" What they say is tremendously informative for you as often they do not know as much as you think. They are talking to you out of respect for the referral source. And it gives you time to think about which direction to take the call.)

- **80%:** the amount of business you'll get **when you are personally introduced.**

Clearly, there are variations on the quality of a personal introduction. Being introduced briefly by chance in the hallway of an office is obviously not as powerful as the three of you scheduling to meet for lunch!

Lessons to Learn:

You don't just want a long list of names of people not expecting your call. (15%) Unless you're a cold calling maestro, you're virtually wasting your time.

Certainly some names that you mention to a referral will carry more weight than others. If these two people have known each other for 25 years, that will help a lot. If the CEO is recommending you to one of her vice presidents, that will make a difference (although still a loaded one). But RARELY does just having a name work as much as we'd like to think. (15%) I am uncomfortable being given just a name and a number because it so seldom leads to business. It never ceases to amaze me how most people think just mentioning their name will make all the difference and how they are usually mistaken!

What you always want to aim for is to ask your referral source (Person A) to warm up their referral (Person B) by talking to him briefly or finding out via e-mail whether he would be interested in a quick conversation. You want someone else to go to bat for you. (50%)

Another advantage to this is you will avoid one of those meetings where someone has agreed to meet you who has NO IDEA what you do and why they're meeting you! (50%)

The best kind of referral to get is without question the personal introduction – lunch, coffee, or beer after hours work best. When someone personally introduces you to a prospect, 80% of the time the business will happen. Why? Because it gives people a chance to get comfortable with you. Their actions speak volumes for your credibility. Clearly, we save these requests for bigger fish. Revisit your prospect list and decide who you would like to meet in person.

The ultimate referral: the personal introduction.

2. Believe 100% in the Benefits of Referrals.

The stronger you believe in building a referral business, the more committed you will be to getting outstanding results.

Why are referrals so great?

Why are they such a wonderful way to build, sustain and grow your business? This is an important refresher so we persist when certain things are not falling into place.

1. **Sometimes you just have to show up sober! A quality referral is the absolute strongest marketing tool you can find: People listen to others when they trust that person's opinion.**

   When someone has given you a really good referral, many of your prospects come pre-sold and all you need to explain is how and when the work can get started. I love these meetings!

2. **Referrals give you more independence and more control over your business.** Why? Because you need people who know, like, and trust you to get referrals. This requires building and maintaining strong relationships. Once you are making a habit of this and you are keeping in touch with your client base, you can always tap into your resource-rich business because you have been making the emotional "bank account deposits" (*see Chapter 2*). This provides the foundation for a stable business which is a much more enjoyable business lifestyle for you.

3. **Working with referrals is about helping others—a client-centered approach—when done right.** The right approach is when your "referral conversation" is focused on your referral source helping people they care about—not some "me, me, me" act of desperation. If that person can see that you are sincerely concerned about the welfare of people they care about, they will take the spirit of your request seriously.

Difficult though this is when you need business yesterday, you need to focus on helping others first. Take that leap of faith and your rewards will come.

The good news is that recent research supports the client-centered approach. In Andy Sernovitz's *Word of Mouth Marketing*, he found that **the two main reasons why others recommend you are because they like to help people they care about and because it makes them feel good!** Neither of these reasons has anything to do with you. Your clients are not motivated to see you drive a nicer car, take more time off, or have plastic surgery!

4. **Referrals are great for people who dislike selling** and aren't very skilled at it. Now someone else is "selling" you beforehand. It allows you to focus on building quality relationships. The business and referrals will come provided you ask for what you want (*see Chapter 4*).

5. **Referrals increase your integrity and enhance your reputation** since new business comes from real people, not clever advertising or marketing gimmicks. Additionally, you won't have to depend on these things to get new business: If you aren't doing a good job, nobody will recommend you. The fact that you get your business from referrals speaks volumes about the quality of your work and what others think of you. Others are putting their integrity on the line to endorse you. That's the kind of business people trust and the kind of endorsement others listen to. It's a wonderful way to be—personally and professionally.

6. **You get to clone your best clients.** Often you get referred to people who have similar personalities to your referral source. Most people will not refer you unless they like you. This is wonderful. If you like your client, the chances are that they'll refer you to people similar to them.

Not long ago I was introduced to the friend of a client. Originally he had told me that if his buddy didn't call me back right away, "tell him Brian will come over and kick his a**!" (I didn't use that line, although I was tempted) I had a hard time keeping a straight face when we met. This friend was remarkably similar in personality: friendly, energetic, talkative, enthusiastic, and he had a good sense of humor. The meeting went great. (See point #1.) Sometimes this feels like the biggest win there is to your referral business.

7. **It's easier to recommend someone else than to "sell yourself":** People listen to third-party endorsements more than you trying to persuade them that you're the best there is. It is one of Robert Cialdini's six universal principles of social influence: the Rule of Authority: we look to experts to show us the way.

8. **It's easier to leverage a good relationship to get business than by advertising, cold calling, or buying leads. (See #1.)**

9. **You can make more money by saving on other marketing expenses.**

10. **It frees up time since you meet with warmer prospects** that are much more likely to do business with you. It is more productive than to spend time with people who are not ready, indecisive, simply kicking tires, or price shopping.

11. **You get measurable results every time.** You know exactly where the business is coming from and where it's not coming from. This awareness allows you to focus on the most productive relationships and organizations that are helping your business the most.

12. **You can feel more peace of mind being more recession proof.** You have a business based on great relationships and people who recommend you to others.

• • •

3. Got Desire?

"The best salespeople we have studied are simply much more motivated than most of the population."

—Benson Smith & Tony Rutigliano,
Discover Your Sales Strengths

Your desire and attitude determine your success level. According to T. Harv Eker in *Secrets of the Millionaire Mind,* what you think about determines how you feel. How you feel determines your actions. Your actions—what you do—determine your results.

The exciting part is that you are totally responsible for your results. How much you want more referrals is going to be the key. You wouldn't be reading this book if you weren't motivated at all. But how much leverage you can get on yourself to take a lot of action—it's truly up to you.

Pain and pleasure determine how much action we take: either how much pain we're experiencing in an area of our life or whether we have a goal or dream that we want so much we're willing to do whatever we can.

It's easy to talk a good game. While who you ARE as a person is most important, your truest values are revealed by what you actually DO—on how you spend your time, not on what you say or have written down on a business plan.

How do you get more motivated to want more referrals?

Try some pain:

Are you missing the boat?

Based on two studies on the financial services industry in 2005 and published in Horsesmouth, LLC's *Automatic Referrals,* the research found that only 11% of clients had been asked for referrals. Yet 72% and 83% of those surveyed said they would happily recommend their advisor but had not been asked. How many of your clients do you ask?

Rule of 20%-60%-20%

Most people get unsolicited referrals from about 20% of their clients. Many salespeople fool themselves into thinking that they have a great referral business because of this 20% even though these two in ten are not being asked for referrals.

I also believe that there are another six in ten (60%) of your clients who would endorse you but need to be asked. They're not thinking about you until you ask. **How many of your clients do you ask?**

If the answer is "none," then **how much more business do you think you could bring in if you asked those 60% effectively?** (It's important to note that you must earn the referral before you ask for it. We'll cover that in an upcoming chapter, so keep reading!)

It's also fair to say that there will usually be one or two in ten (10-20%) who just aren't going to recommend you. Maybe they can be turned around in time but they may well be unnecessary "projects."

Try some pleasure:

First, I suggest that you re-read section #2. Soak up the benefits. Second, if your referral business is coming from 20% of your clients and you're hardly asking any of them, what would your business look like if another 6 in 10 (60%) of your clients were recommending you?

Not every referral is created equal. I am not going to claim you'll see a 300% increase in business. Ultimately, there will still likely be an 80-20 Law in most cases (where you're getting 80% of your business from 20% of the people you know). But until you've asked everyone who is happy with your work (or is considered a "go-to" reference person or friend)—what could that untapped potential be? And if a lot more people send you business, that 80-20 spread is going to be much higher up the scale from your present situation!

Set some exciting referral goals: it's what it makes OF you that matters most, not what it makes for you.

Why? Because it is who you become that matters most. You will stretch yourself and think bigger. Your confidence will grow from facing your fears.

These goals need not focus on money. For most people it's better if they don't. Focus on helping more people, on results in other parts of your life, and getting better at what you do in measurable ways. Good goals can simply be about implementing the 6 Steps to a Fearless Referral Conversation (*see Chapter* 6).

Doing the unrealistic is easier than doing the realistic.

Author Tim Ferriss points out in his book, *The 4-Hour Work Week,* that you will have more success aiming higher for two reasons:

a) **99% of people are "convinced they are incapable of achieving great things" so they never try. That means there are very few people going for gold. If everyone else feels insecure, you don't need to be the one selling yourself short.**

b) When you do have an ambitious target, it gets your adrenaline going and you think of more creative solutions. ***"It's as easy as believing it can be done."***

Motivation is What Top Entrepreneurs All Have in Common

While in England on a recent trip, I picked up David Lester's highly informative *How They Started: How 30 Good Ideas Became Great Businesses*.

In his introduction, Lester notes that almost everyone on the planet has an idea or two for a business; it's just that most people don't pursue that idea—and fewer still succeed.

While they all BEHAVED in similar ways—it was how they went about growing their business that made the difference. And **at first there was little monetary reward.**

For many months, and even years, very little of the money made was spent on themselves. Quite a few of the 30 people featured worked part-time on their business until they thought they could take the leap.

They all focused on one idea. They all kept it simple. Yes, eighteen hour days were pretty common because starting momentum takes a great deal of effort and commitment. "None of the founders started out as workaholics—they all began as normal people just like you."

But also key was they kept trying and believing.

About half of the businesses in the book had weak sales early on and had to wait much longer than they expected for business to pick up. **Every business in the book** ***"had to overcome significant issues to keep trading, let alone succeed; along the way, each founder faced doubt, anxiety, stress and pressure level way beyond what most employees face; their ability to cope with this, almost always deeply rooted in strong self belief, was an important factor in why they succeeded where so many businesses haven't."***

They had motivation, passion, and commitment. This is what you need to improve your referral business.

NONE of the business owners interviewed set out to become wealthy. None of them! Their motives ranged from wanting a livelihood after being laid off, to wanting to create a higher quality product or service not then available, to wanting to see if they could make it in a new market. ***"To work the hours, take the risks, make the personal life sacrifices all the founders have done, takes very, very strong motivation; very few people who say they want to build a business in order to get rich have anything like that degree of motivation."***

Lester concludes that it wasn't about being from the right stock or wanting more money that drove these businesses to succeed. They had a focused idea for a product or service that some part of the world needed. ***"And they needed literally extra-ordinary levels of passion, energy, self belief and stamina, the ability and desire to focus, and a good measure of judgment."***

My final point here, and arguably the most important, is that your motivation comes most profoundly and lasts longer when tied to your sense of purpose – why you were put on this earth. Connecting to that will take you where you want to go. Brian Souza's *Become Who You Were Born to Be* does a marvelous job of addressing this. I sincerely wish you all a healthy dose of these qualities so you get the referrals and the results you want!

• • •

4. Deliberate Practice.

> *"Happy people ...don't wait for events or other people to make them happy. They're not passive victims."*
>
> —Dan Baker

Ever catch yourself thinking about someone who produces more than you and saying: "he's a natural," or "she's a lot smarter than me," or "that person is so much more experienced than I am"?

According to the research reported in Geoff Colvin's recent *Talent is Overrated*, those reasons aren't valid. Look around you:

Top performers are NOT generally:

- **Naturally gifted:** Most of the people who became the most accomplished in their field *"did not show early evidence of gifts."*
- **Exclusively hard workers:** We all know people who work plenty of hours who achieve average results.
- **More experienced:** We all know people with more experience than us who get average results
- **Higher in IQ:** We all know people who are smarter than us who get average results
- **Born with great memories:** Do you get the point?!

And believing these things simply gives people an excuse to be mediocre.

1. **The key message in this book is that superior performers pursue DELIBERATE PRACTICE in areas that address specific skills that take them AROUND their limitations. This is what you need to do to get high-quality referrals on a consistent basis.**
   One great sports example is Jerry Rice, the former San Francisco 49er (since most of us have not been professional athletes, look for the concepts here). The records he holds are not 5 or 10 percent higher than the person in second place (which would still be impressive) but 50%! He played 20 seasons—until he was 42—in a position where the average player does not make it to age 30. Yet he was not considered fast by professional standards.

   Rice's success came "because he worked harder in practice and in the off-season than anyone else" and **because he designed his practice to work on his specific needs.** He focused intently on the four things he had to excel in to compensate for his lack of speed: running precise patterns (strength training); explosive acceleration (uphill wind sprints); endurance training for stamina late in games; and changing directions suddenly without signaling his intent (trail running).

   His off-season training regimen was considered so brutal that his coaches refused to share it with anyone for fear that others might damage themselves!
   The point here is that it's not just graft that gets you places; it's the right kind of practice activity that can help you get better results. The same is true for getting more referrals. What are you doing to improve your game?

2. **The crucial question to think through is: what's the most important activity for making me better at what I do?**
   In general, do you need to practice:
   - How you run your first appointments so they lead to more meetings?
   - How you make prospecting calls?
   - Look at the results you get from asking for referrals (which is a specific skill you can practice), Do you need to:

- Increase your networking activities and coffees with potential centers of influence? Could they be sending you more referrals? The likely answer is yes.
- Join someone you know who runs meetings well and learn from them?
- Change the wording that you use?
- Create a meeting agenda so you don't run out of time?

The only way to be more effective prospecting, getting referrals or as a networker is to pinpoint your weaknesses and work around them. Learn more about what the most effective producers do.

3. **Superior performers perceive more, know more, and remember more.**
   They notice things average performers do not; they look further ahead for trends; they know more from seeing less; they are more expert in their field because they study more; their ability to recall and interpret information is superior, too; they see themselves as responsible for the things that do not go well; they are always getting better; and they are always overstraining themselves mentally.

   Most of these things you can decide to start doing more of today too!

4. **Getting there is tough but is available to almost anyone:**
   "Landing on your butt twenty thousand times is where great performance comes from."
   The highest achievers in any field have accumulated many more lifetime hours of practice than everyone else. Colvin calls it the Ten-year Rule (ten years before you can become acclaimed) which is rather similar to what author and journalist Malcolm Gladwell has called the 10,000 Hour Rule. This is the dominant reason why so-called child prodigies appear to be innately talented. Tiger Woods' father had a metal golf club in his son's hands from the age of 7 MONTHS and on a golf course at 2 years old! Mozart's father had his son on a program of intensive training in composition and performing at age 3.

5. **The chief constraint is MENTAL for those who also want to be high achievers and get more referrals.**
   You won't make any progress if you work hard and then just do things in your comfort zone. You need to step outside your comfort zone regularly and face your fears.

   University of Michigan business professor Noel Tichy has identified three areas: the comfort zone (useless), the learning zone (great) and, beyond that, the panic zone (unproductive). To become top of your game, you must be getting in your learning zone as much as possible *"and then forcing (yourself) to stay continuously in it as it changes, which is even harder—these are the first and most important characteristics of deliberate practice."*

   The great mental intangible to sustaining this is your motivation. Colvin reports that most researchers believe that this drive must be primarily *intrinsic* because of the sacrifices necessary to be the best. It is founded in people's desire to solve a great question or problem in their field (enjoying their focus on the process not the outcome/goal), to do good in the world, to make progress, to be the best, be an achiever or desire power.

   A great example of this is that most eminent executives and entrepreneurs keep working long after they need to. What do you think was the first thing Bill Cosby did when he sold the rights to The Cosby Show for $25,000,000? Take a month off and sit on the beach? Party in Paris? No, he took a red eye flight to Vegas so he could test out some new material in a stand-up routine for his next project.

   When is extrinsic motivation effective? At times, recognition and feedback can really help provided that the feedback is constructive, nonthreatening and work-focused— rather than person-focused.

6. **Much of this boils down to what you want in life, what you believe you're capable of doing, and the belief that your work will pay off.**
   ***Passion develops over time* based on how much action you take (not on waiting for it).** The "Eureka" moment of a genius

idea is mostly a myth and generally comes after years of intensive preparation.

7. **Support, feedback, repetition, and activity designed to improve performance.**
"No one becomes extraordinary on his own." Especially at critical times in their development, Colvin recommends the importance of an outside eye to see the things you cannot not see about yourself.

"It's apparent why becoming significantly good at almost anything is extremely difficult without the help of a teacher or coach, at least in the early going." He says there's a reason why the best golfers still work with coaches. (*See Chapter 7 on the team you need to get you to the top.*) A supportive environment matters.

Last, Colvin does say that NOTHING can fully explain achievement because "real life is too complicated for that." However, clearly there is much that can be done by each of us to move beyond being average and aiming to make more of a difference and ultimately becoming one of the best in our field. Getting better at bringing in more referrals is a great place to focus.

• • •

5. The Three "Musts" for Me to Help You

a) **Don't reinvent the wheel**

Within the realms of your own values and common sense, follow the suggestions in this book. As humans, we innately believe we can and should come up with our own solutions.

The challenging reality is that this belief is often false. Unfortunately, we overestimate our abilities and do not realize that we are average at most things. Harvard psychology professor Daniel Gilbert's research is just one recent example of social science finding that we do a TERRIBLE job of evaluating ourselves: we typically overrate our abilities and underestimate our knowledge. We tend to seek out information that already supports what we believe and we tend to discount information that contradicts it!

The statistics are quite hilarious. For example, one study found that 90% of drivers consider themselves to be safer than average. 94% of college professors consider themselves to be above average educators! However, only 50% can actually be above average, and the other 50% below average. One research team mentioned in Gilbert's book, *Stumbling on Happiness,* concluded that *"Most of us appear to believe that we are more athletic, intelligent, organized, ethical, logical, interesting, fair-minded, and healthy – not to mention attractive—than the average person."*

We rely on our own (flawed) memory and imagination rather than follow those who have been there and done it**. We are more likely to make our own mistakes rather than learn from those who have already made them. You do not need to do that with getting referrals.** Because we see ourselves as so unique, we often think that the experiences of others do not apply to us. Most of the time, this is not true.

What does this all mean? It means that you need to work harder—but it's equally important to work smarter. Don't try to reinvent the wheel. Instead, apply what you learn from this book and from others to develop your skills. This content has been tried and tested over many years with thousands of people. Don't resist implementing ideas that work for others. The very fact that others have done it is proof you can do it too – not proof you should buck the trend because that's how you live your life!

However: DO make these ideas your own!

Tweak them to fit your personality and communication style. If you read an example and say to yourself; "I would never say that!" Then pause and ask yourself how you might re-word it to make the same point.

b) Be coachable

I'm guessing you wouldn't have picked up this book if you weren't open to new ideas. However, you'll only be able to successfully increase your referral business if you act on new ideas. Your key to gaining referrals is action, persistence, and perseverance. Avoid just "trying" something once and then convincing yourself that it doesn't work. I have confidence that you're going to e-mail me with your success stories, because I know that the strategies in this book work. It just takes discipline.

Very few people are willing to: a) customize content to make it suit your personality; b) be open-minded to some new ideas; and c) persist—because it may not all happen overnight.

Being coachable isn't as easy as you might hope. Most salespeople and business owners pride themselves on their independence, and this often includes the notion that they can figure pretty much everything out themselves. This is a strong quality and it will take you to good, even to above average, but it will not take you to great. I did not see this in my life until relatively recently. Then I opened my eyes and realized that all high achievers reach out for support, guidance, and (often) coaching. It is not a coincidence that all top performers work with qualified coaches—golfers, cyclists, writers, and speakers. Nor is it a coincidence that the middle-class millionaires researched in Russ Alan Prince's 2008 book of the same name hire the best coaches, consultants, and advisors to help them play a better game in whatever work they pursue.

I just ask that you be aware that as you read this you're not out to prove that parts of this can't work for you because you're different or your business is different! Getting referrals is not that complicated, and if you think it is, that may well be your defense mechanism to keep success away from you. (You might want to read that again)

Finally, if what you're doing right now works really well for you, then keep doing it if it's ethical! If you're a manager and you want to train others to do the same, go ahead *provided it works as well for them*! That's a big caveat because often things don't translate so well.

c) **Persist**

> *If I had to select one quality, one personal characteristic that I regard as being most highly correlated with success, whatever the field, I would pick the trait of persistence.*
>
> —Richard DeVos, Amway Co-founder

Numbers rarely lie. A study I found in Jack Canfield's *The Success Principles* shares work done by Herbert True at Notre Dame that demonstrates how incredibly important it is simply never to give up.

His research of salespeople found that
44% gave up after 1 request to do business
24% gave up after 2 requests
14% gave up after 3 requests
12% gave up after 4 requests.

So 94% of them gave up after asking four times for the business. In other words, only 6% really persisted. 6%! But here's the really dramatic part:

60% of all sales are made after the fourth call.

Is it any wonder that the top 6% of salespeople make so much more money than the rest?

• • •

6. It's Easier Than Learning Italian!

> *"While one person hesitates because he feels inferior, the other is busy making mistakes and becoming superior."*
>
> —Henry C. Link

Getting referrals is a learned skill!

Don't you just have to ask? "Ask" is usually the first word that comes up when I ask an audience what it takes to get referrals. Yes, you almost always need to ask. However, it's not just about "asking." It's not just about getting a bunch of names of random people. That's why I say getting referrals is a learned skill. It takes some time and practice to consistently be referred to people who are quality prospects, expecting your call, and looking forward to hearing from you. That's a good referral.

Most people think that getting referrals *should be* pretty easy to do. But for most people it's not. It's got more in common with learning a foreign language or new skill such as golf or carpentry. In other words, for most of us we're going to start out trying one or two basic things to get more referrals. The more we practice it, the more we will learn and the more fluent we will get. Our confidence then starts to grow and we are more open to identifying the remaining areas where we still need to improve to get more referrals.

The point is: it's a learning process that takes time, not a one-time event. You don't attend one seminar or read one book and master getting referrals. You take away a few points, work on them, keep learning and revisiting all the ideas. One step at a time, you implement them into your business. Ideally, you work with a partner, mentor, manager, or coach to get you there (*see Chapter* 7).

There are two main reasons why this learning process is a misunderstood concept:

1. **We mistakenly believe getting referrals should come quite naturally to us**. I believe it's similar to the skill of listening or

providing great customer service. We think of them as things that we just do and do quite well. Yet if we asked the people who know us, the reality may be quite different! They may say that we interrupt too much or don't seem to pay full attention. We may not realize that our eye contact is erratic when someone is speaking to us or that we would struggle to paraphrase what that person said to us.

We have the same misconception about referrals. We believe that somehow it should be fairly easy to get them and then get discouraged quickly because it is not.

The same is likely true for our customer service. I have met so many business owners who think their service is what sets them apart from their competition. Think about this. It's impossible! Think about your daily experiences. Do most businesses wow you with their great customer service? No! It is a rare occasion when you walk out of a store or business thinking "that place had really good service—they were really friendly people!" The hard part is that even after reading this, you're still probably thinking that you're the exception who is a great listener and has top-notch customer service! Referrals are the same way.

2. **We all know one fearless salesperson that seems to find ways to ask for and get referrals all the time. We all know a business that appears to run seamlessly on referrals from people who aren't even asked.** Stop for a second and ask yourself exactly how many people really fit that description. Are you sure it's 100% accurate even for that one person? How long did it take for her to accomplish this? Often this is partly a reputation or perception that this person has, and he says nothing to diminish it even if it's not entirely accurate!

Second, there are MANY reasons why a business gets to this point, and this book will address them throughout. Rather like being a good listener and having great customer service, there are people who—for whatever reason—are very good in these areas. Some of them are naturals (at some of the things discussed in this book); some of them are just plain more likeable; and others have worked very hard to get there, are more detail-oriented, and follow-up more promptly.

Forget about wishing you were a natural. Be yourself and start making progress! For most people **getting referrals is like learning Italian. It's a skill that needs to be learned.** When we accept this, then we can have more realistic expectations about making progress one step at a time and getting more referrals. The good news is that it's easier than learning Italian.

Getting Referrals is not an overnight success.
One of the biggest myths in our culture is that "successful" people are naturals and that their "overnight" success was virtually preordained. Yet if you read most people's actual life story, you learn that it was not a cake walk at all and that they slogged away for many years developing their skills and expertise. The truth behind most highly accomplished people is that they have fallen on their faces more times than everyone else, but they kept getting up AND they have learned from and used their failures well.

It's also time to accept that the asking for referrals will probably be done badly at first—just as if you were learning Italian or like the first few times you got behind the wheel of a car. And that's okay. It is all a process, a new habit. Certainly this is why role playing with others will make such a big difference.

The only way to get good at asking for referrals is to practice it and accept that the first few times will feel awkward. It is not going to be seamless and comfortable. There is no other way! Get used to the slight discomfort. You may be starting out at square one.

Lastly, if you're a manager or owner, it's okay to admit you're not perfect in front of your salespeople! Do you expect everyone you hire to be perfect? Get the load off your shoulders and tell your sales team: "I have expertise in many areas." Feel free to list those areas. It will make you feel better and more real when you then say: "There is one area though where I need to improve too and that's why over the next 12 months I've committed to work with you on getting more referrals." Your sales team already knows anyway. You might well be more respected for conceding that you too, on occasion, have human qualities!

• • •

7. More Friends = More Referrals: Master the L-Factor and the Comfort Factor.

"Our nation is so focused on efficiency and productivity that we forget that likeability is truly our lifeline."

—Tim Sanders, *The Likeability Factor*

"Before you do anything, make the other person comfortable."

—Harry Beckwith, *You, Inc.*

Last summer I was in Canada having lunch with my cousin, the owner of a fairly unique branding and design business called Breakhouse. He, an interior designer, and his business partner, an architect, turn retail stores into a 'Starbucks-type experience' and tie it into the new company brand. He was telling me that they had recently landed their biggest client to date: Bell Canada, the Canadian equivalent to AT&T or the UK's British Telecom. Apparently their retail sales had dropped from first to third in the country, and so they were working on a new corporate image.

My favorite question to ask people is to trace how they got the business. He explained that they had worked with a local telecom company in eastern Canada and this work had won an award. The company referred them to Bell Canada. That's right, Breakhouse doesn't advertise. All their business comes from referrals.

Three other companies were vying for the business: Goliaths by comparison—two from New York and one from the Netherlands. Two of these other companies have 500 employees; the other has an international client list to die for. "So how did you beat these guys out?" I had to know. I don't want to oversimplify my point. He cited two or three reasons. Their proposal was impressive and he was pretty sure they had put more effort into it than their competitors. They were Canadian; he wasn't sure if that had helped or not. "But you know what I think it was? I think they just liked us more. My business partner is a pretty funny guy. He's good at connecting with people and loosening them up. We just hit it off."

This reminds me of a coffee I had with a mortgage consultant that I've known for about six years. She used to network everywhere and was excellent at both giving and asking for referrals. I know I learned some things from her. Then 10 months before I saw her, she became pregnant. Due to her diabetes, was unable to drive for eight months. Her face-to-face networking abruptly stopped. Yet she was still getting a lot of referrals coming in. When I asked her what she was doing to maintain relationships, she told me. It was the same kind of stuff every mortgage professional I've ever met does: send out rate updates and help prepare flyers for open houses. I was really puzzled. This activity was not setting her apart at all.

Then it clicked. What she has is the Likeability-Factor. She treats everyone like they are her best friend. She has mastered how to be genuinely pleased to see you. You can see it on her face and you can hear it in her voice on the phone. It is sincere and, while it sounds like common sense, we know this is rare. Think about it for a moment: who do you know who does this consistently? She knows how people want to be treated and she does it when she doesn't feel like it. This had helped her sustain her success.

It's not that we don't already know all this; it's why don't we run our businesses based on the L-Factor all the time?

Why do we sometimes prospect people we don't much care for and who treat us like one of those bugs flying around on the inside of our windshield when we have the windows rolled up and the a/c blasting?

Do you focus your prospecting and client retention efforts on your top 20%—the ones who will inevitably refer you the most?

What is the L-Factor?

Former Yahoo executive Tim Sanders wrote *The Likeability Factor* in 2005, and it is full of research that supports the feeling we all have that people want to do business with and associate with others they know, like and trust. These are the people we want to refer. Again, what are you doing about it? Sales guru Jeffrey Gitomer's advice? *"Win sales based on friendship, not price. Be friendly first."*

Be Real.

Others call this authenticity. Sanders argues that people need to be able to read your feelings. Failing to connect can make it difficult to get a business relationship off the ground. And you WILL get fewer referrals. People will go to bat for you more when they really like you.

Four Outstanding Tips About the L-Factor Worth Sharing from Jeffrey Gitomer: Read this more than once and live it!

1. ***"I put value in the hands of my potential customers before I ever ask them to buy anything."***
   Anyone who has heard me present or been coached by me hears me emphasize this point over and over. Bring as much value to a client meeting up front regardless of whether it has anything to do with your business. It will set you apart very quickly. Why? Because it shows you care, it takes a little effort and most people won't take the time.

2. Make friends before you start, or don't start.
   "I don't win sales on price. I win sales on friendship."

3. Act professionally, speak friendly.
   Gitomer has made me realize that sometimes I am too stiff because somehow I think it will raise my credibility and that I do not always focus on the L-Factor. Instead I run the risk of being seen as a cardboard box. *"I try to act as professionally as I can, but I always err on the side of being too friendly."* This also allows him to ask for a higher price and get it.

   Another thought: I like to get down to business because I know people are busy. This overlooks the people who want to "connect" first. I risk losing that business.

I learned an interesting point from Britain's best-known magician, Paul Daniels. He observed in an interview that real experts are "light" with their subject matter and don't feel the need to take themselves too seriously. This takes time to develop. He's not suggesting such people don't speak with eloquence and earnestness. I think he's saying that they don't live in fear that one day they are going to get "found out" as not really being credible. They are comfortable in their own skin.

4. ***"If you make a sale, you earn a commission. If you make a friend, you can earn a fortune.***
   This philosophy is rarely used in sales. Those who employ it are the top performers and the top salespeople. They build relationships. I challenge you that this is the single hardest lesson to learn and at the same time, it is the single most powerful and most financially rewarding lesson that I teach."

More friends=more referrals!

Four Final Thoughts on this topic:

a) The wildly underestimated comfort factor:

Author Harry Beckwith, a renowned expert on brand positioning and corporate branding strategies has conducted much research on "the Comfort Factor." In his enormously helpful book, *You, Inc.*, he found that when it comes to finding the best of the best, people do not really know what the best company is for any industry. No one can be sure that their service providers are necessarily the best—it's very subjective.

Who can say which car or brand of jeans is the best on the market? Can you look others in the eye and tell them your veterinarian or Realtor is without doubt the best in the country?

Why do people continue to do business with personal service firms? According to Beckwith, "Their answer is one word. You hear this word from clients more than all their words combined. The word is '*comfort*'."

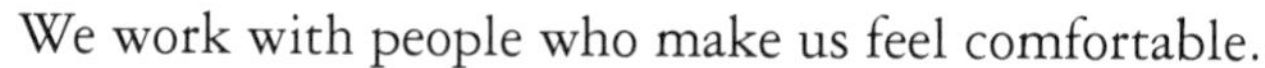

We work with people who make us feel comfortable.

b) **The Law of Attraction.** According to Gallup research, 99% of people would rather spend time with positive people who make them feel good. Typically if you don't like yourself all that much, you are unlikely to attract many others because you will not be instilling confidence in them. Both Jack Canfield and Nathaniel Brandon have terrific resources on this topic both listed in the bibliography.

c) **Show more compassion.** In *Love is the Killer App,* best-selling author Tim Sanders urges us to be more human: "*Most of us don't feel comfortable with workplace intimacy. But I say you've got to express your compassion, because, combined with knowledge and (your) network, it is the way we win hearts and influence business in this, the dawn of the new business world.*"

d) **Finally, truly enjoy what you do.** Richard Branson's motto is "have fun, work hard, and the money will come." It's hard to fake people out for long. How can you expect referrals if you have little real enthusiasm for what you're doing? One of my favorite sayings is you have two choices in life if you don't like something: change what you're doing or change how you look at it. To get fired up about what you do, it often revolves around helping others and making a difference. How do you do that and is it fulfilling enough?

You spend so many hours working that it is crucial you enjoy what you do.

• • •

8. More friends = More Referrals: The Rule of Liking

> *"The more we like people, the more we want to say yes to them."*
>
> —Robert Cialdini's *Rule of Liking*

Arizona State professor Robert Cialdini has been studying the field of social influence for over 35 years. The Rule of Liking is one of his six universal principles. In his 1984 classic, *Influence: The Psychology of Persuasion*, he talks about Joe Girard, considered the "greatest car salesman" by the Guinness Book of World Records. He sold five cars or trucks *every day he worked*!! When asked how this happened, Girard simply said that people had found someone they liked to buy from and a fair price.

From a referral standpoint, the question to ask yourself is, 'what can I do to be more liked by this person?' This truly is pivotal because the rule states that the more people like us, the more they want to help us.

Cialdini found five areas that often help us be better liked by others:

1. Physical attractiveness

He cites studies from the political, legal, human resources, and educational fields that indicate startling findings: We often vote for the candidate we find more attractive; we often hire the people we find more attractive; lighter sentences and more favorable verdicts for damages are awarded to more attractive people, and school teachers are more lenient with more attractive students.

I know that *you* certainly wouldn't let such a thing influence you! Cialdini argues these things often happen unconsciously and automatically.

OK, you don't need to have plastic surgery, but at least think hard about your health habits and dress code. Author Brian Tracy notes that he was shocked when he realized that many of the triathlon and marathon runners he knew were also the highest achievers in their fields.

2. Similarity

Since most of us are average-looking (not you, of course – you're in the top 10%, right?!), there is still hope: *"We like people who are similar to us."* This can vary from opinions, personalities, background, lifestyle, age, religion, politics, and the way we dress to seemingly trivial similarities, such as the rock bands we liked when we were 14.

John H. Johnson, who was born in a tin-roof shack in Arkansas in 1918, was the founder of *Ebony* magazine and the first black American on the *Forbes* magazine list of the 400 richest people in the U.S.A. Whenever he was to meet someone for the first time, he would do his research to find a similarity: *"I want to know where they came from, what are their interests, what can I talk to them about. You have to establish rapport with people, and you establish rapport by having mutual interests and mutual knowledge of each other."*

It is very difficult to sell anything to someone if you have no common ground.

DO IT! Taking the time in meetings to find more common ground with others now looks a whole lot smarter. Make a stronger connection! How conscientiously do you do this?

3. Compliments

So what else did Joe Girard do to make such remarkable sales? He sent greeting cards *every month* to the 13,000 plus people in his network. Inside the card were three words: *"I like you,"* and his signature.

Now, this was the 1970s and, if you're like me, you're thinking "that's so corny and transparent." Cialdini believes otherwise: *"Joe understands an important fact about human nature: we are phenomenal suckers for flattery."*

DO IT! No, not false praise, but it is time to ask yourself how often you say nice things to others and how often you are keeping in touch with your clients in a way that makes *them* feel good. One solution I have created for business owners and salespeople to add a consistent positive touch is a Chicken Soup for the Soul-style, hassle-free monthly e-newsletter. If you're curious to see what that is, check out the appendix page: *The Loyalty E-zine*.

4. Contact and cooperation

Frequent Contact: we do not realize how much we are influenced by exposure to something on a repeated basis—this is why you will get more business (including referrals) from people if you keep your name in front of them year-round.

Cooperating with others on a common project or for a specific cause can be a powerful reason for liking. This is supported by Thomas J. Stanley's research discussed in *Networking with Millionaires*: *"People see you at your best when you are doing something for a charitable cause."* You are so much more likely to make deeper connections through non-profit work or with the same professional association than by meeting someone at a business after-hours because you have more commitment invested in the same project. These deeper bonds are more likely to lead to referral relationships.

I recently saw a high-producing financial advisor from Boston speak who said that every month he would identify the 25 people who had the biggest impact on his business. The last time he had done this he had found that 17 of them were people he had met through his volunteer work with the Make-a-Wish foundation.

5. Positive and negative association

Negative Association: you've heard the phrase "kill the messenger." After years of poking fun at meteorologists, I had no idea that it was not unusual for them to receive hate mail—and worse—because of their predictions. People have blamed them for spoiling travel plans, crops, basements, weddings, and almost everything else under the sun.

Here's a true story too funny not to share from David Langford of Associated Press:

"Tom Bonner, 35, who has been with KARK-TV in Little Rock, Ark, for 11 years, remembers the time a burly farmer from Lonoke, with too much to drink, walked up to him in a bar, poked a finger in his chest, and said: "You're the one that sent that tornado and tore my house up. I'm going to take your head off.

"Bonner said he looked for the bouncer, couldn't spot him, and replied, "That's right about the tornado, and I'll tell you something else, I'll send another one if you don't back off."

Positive Association: This is why products use celebrities to endorse them – sales increase; it's why products call themselves the "official" hair spray/deodorant/checking account of the US Olympic Team. Irrationally the product has more credibility so we like it more. It's why companies use attractive models to enhance what they're selling.

Two other interesting additional revelations:

a) Politicians and fundraisers know that people will approve of you more (and give you more money) after you have fed them a nice meal. Feeding people can boost likeability.

b) Some people are fanatical about their favorite sports teams; sharing a love for the same team can boost your Likeability-Factor. Somehow, that team starts to represent you and prove your superiority – when they win. It is highly amusing to note that most people say the following after a game:
When your team wins, you say "WE won!"
When your team loses, you say, "THEY lost."

DO IT! This is one reason why it is always wise to speak positively and optimistically about your business or company. Other people want to associate with winners.

As a reminder: for more referrals, the question to ask yourself is, "What can I do to be more liked by this person?" Use the ideas above because the more people like you, the more they want to help you.

Likeability: the art of finding that jugular emotional connection.

CHAPTER 2:

Earning the Fearless Referral

"Our only real economic security lies in our power to meet human needs; (it) does not lie in our organizations or our jobs."

—Stephen Covey, *The 8th Habit*

Before you start asking clients for referrals, there are some rules you need to consider.

1. You Only Ask for Referrals If You've Earned Them!

"Money is merely a reward for solving problems."

—Mike Murdock

Too much of what we hear about referrals is based around techniques: how to ask, when to ask, what to say, and who to get them from. We don't spend enough time focusing on WHAT we are actually doing to earn the word-of-mouth recommendation.

Let's look at some word-of-mouth facts highlighted in Andy Sernovitz' Word of Mouth Marketing:

1. People don't talk about the ordinary.

Have you ever recommended that someone eat at Perkins or Burger King? Pizza Hut? Ever told a friend they should try Coca Cola? No. It's too ordinary.

How do your clients see you? Is it possible many of your clients see you as business as usual? Most salespeople will say no to this—after all, nobody thinks they are ordinary. But how often do you walk out of a business/store/restaurant saying to yourself: "That place had really good service!"? Not very often, right? Are you sure you're that much better and provide significantly better service than your competition?

Are you sure you're actually earning referrals?

Ask yourself: What do I need to do to earn more referrals? What would be extraordinary? How can I provide more value or better service?

Mull this over for the rest of the week!

2. **When people's expectations are met, they do NOT talk about it to others.**

When you go to the dentist, you expect him or her to take care of your teeth. When you take your dog to the vet, you expect him to get well. If you hire someone to service your air conditioning, you expect it to run better after that person leaves.

My point? Simply doing your job isn't enough. You must exceed expectations.

We don't apply this thinking to our own clients and our own business enough.

Ask yourself: Why should someone recommend you? Why would anyone new want to work with you?

Because our brains are wired to think about ourselves 95% of the time, we somehow assume that our service is better than everyone else's—even if it isn't. At almost every networking event I've ever been to, someone earnestly tells me that the unique part of his business is the customer service. This gets pretty meaningless after a while.

If you really want more referrals, you must truly EXCEED expectations.

Ask yourself: What else can I do that will exceed my clients' expectations? Can you provide information that helps him in another area of his business? What can you do to help your client even if it goes outside the realm of your expertise?

3. It's more important to be different than it is to be better.

People don't talk about what's best, they talk about what's different. Here are a few examples:

Jeffrey Gitomer has branded himself as the top sales authority in the USA. Is he really? His content is very good, and he's branded himself marvelously as different – funny, creative, not a "suit." It seems to resonate well with people.

Is Larry Winget really one of the best motivational speakers in the USA? He dresses like a biker. He looks different than all his competition. He has successfully branded himself as an in-your-face type of guy. He knows his stuff. Does he know more than anyone else?

John Eliot is a professor at Rice University who writes and speaks on peak performance. He has branded himself differently not by his appearance or marketing savvy, but by stating his opinions to catch people's attention: goal setting is for couch potatoes; hard work is overrated; stress is a good thing. It got me to read his book (once I saw his credentials) and it is full of great research and ideas.

Yes, these guys are all good, but what makes them stand out is what makes them different.

Differentiating yourself doesn't have to be world changing. It could be making an initially powerful impact when people first walk into your place of business. Some banks and car dealerships now have Starbucks machines in them. That was once a wow factor.

Perhaps you differentiate yourself through excellent follow-up and keeping in touch. Trent, a Realtor I know well, does this better than anyone I've ever met. Think about how many people want your business but don't keep in touch like they care about you? I got one e-mail after I spent almost $40,000 on a car a year or so ago. Not even a call. I've bought three properties in my lifetime. Only one of the Realtors I worked with kept in regular contact. Would you refer someone who didn't even follow up to say thank you?

Ask yourself: What can you do that's different from your competition?

4. It's not customer service; it's customer surprises that count.

I say this to emphasize that "business as usual" nets zero referrals. Great customer service matters greatly, but what people remember most are the nice surprises. Last weekend I opened my mailbox to find that someone who had been to a recent seminar of mine had sent me a book. (This is a very quick way to win my heart!) And it wasn't a book about her business; it wasn't some vague ruse to sell me something. On the contrary, it was a book she knew I would really want to read. Every time I see that book, I remember who gave it to me. Bottles of wine are nice, but they get consumed quickly. That book will be a reference tool for as long as I live.

Here are other real life examples of people I've worked with as referral coaching clients or met at seminars who earn many referrals:

- An insurance agent who takes one weekend/year and makes quilts for the clients who have the most policies with her;
- Two mortgage consultants who offer you water, coffee *or beer* when you arrive (and mean it!);
- An insurance agent who has a community notice board where locals can advertise for a baby sitter, sell a boat, or promote a yard sale;
- A Realtor who routinely gives away fresh eggs, homemade jam, and just-made maple syrup;
- A financial advisor who regularly invites his best clients to Red Sox, Patriots, and Celtics games.

Ask yourself: What can I do so that my clients remember me after a meeting?

Remember: Your goal is to make your clients happy. What are you doing to achieve this? When you make them happy, that's when they'll talk about you and refer you to others.

5. Keep filling up the wells with water.

Referrals do not come out of thin air or thin relationships: You can't get water out of an empty well.

Ask yourself: What are you doing to build and nurture important relationships from all the people who could be referring you?

(See sections 2, 3, and 4 in this chapter for more on this!)

6. Get your clients talking about their passions. Better yet, help them to connect more to what they love.

Former president of the Word of Mouth Marketing Association, George Silverman, said, *"People talk about their passions. You can't get them to shut up about their passions."*

Think about yourself here. You love talking about your kids, your favorite team, a hobby, your pet, favorite band, or vacation destination. **Your clients like you more when they know you care enough to ask them about theirs.**

One of the reasons I like my vet so much is he is one of the few people outside my family who *sincerely* asks me about two of the things I care about most: my business and my dog. Kurt, one of my past clients, always used to ask me about Coventry City, my favorite team, even though it rarely feels good to talk about them because they are pretty inconsistent! I still appreciated him remembering.

Maybe your client is not that interested in what you do professionally. Just as you may not be very interested in what they do. So know what they DO care about most and talk to them about that!

Does everyone out there know exactly what they want in life? Does everyone out there have all the time they want to connect to their passions? Here are some ways to help your clients reconnect with their passions:

a) **Host client events that revolve around something your clients love.** Bring people together who have the same strong interests in life. They will talk to each other and you will initiate great word-of-mouth about you! That's one reason why target marketing works so well (all people with a common interest).

- A business owner friend of mine has several events each year at Green Bay Packer and Milwaukee Brewer games.
- A florist friend of mine hosts a variety of events on gardening, interior design, creative gift ideas and floral design followed by a 15% off everything in the store before they leave.
- A financial advisor former client of mine has hosted events at a microbrewery where clients and guests get a tour and great beer-tasting experience. How easy do you suppose it is for his clients to invite friends to that?!

b) **Be a resource to your clients.** Do you know the best resources in town who may be able to help your clients? The more people you know professionally who have different specialties, the more you can become a resource to your clients. (Additionally, by referring others, in turn, they are much more likely to refer you—my next book will address how to master this.) This is a way to position yourself as a "go to" person and build trust with clients.

Almost everyone has money worries at times – do you know people who can help your clients in those areas? Know a good travel agent or travel website for your client wanting to get away in the winter? Do you know a massage therapist for your stressed client? How about a friend who has connections to get tickets for sporting events or knows about the best plays or bands coming to town? The list is endless. Create more traffic through you. Create more buzz. Very few professionals have that reputation—why not be that person? It's word-of-mouth, remember?

c) **Provide a newsletter for your clients to help them connect to what matters most in their lives.** This is valuable information that most people would welcome. They'd be happy to hear from you and, as importantly, it is something they will talk about. A few weeks ago a client of mine sent me a You Tube video from an Oprah show. The content of this was so moving that I wrote to two people close to me about how much I loved them. This is not typical behavior for me! (I only told my dad once right before he died.) I got a fabulous response from both people. This person made a difference in my life. Do you suppose I'm trying even harder to help this client get more referrals? (See Appendix for more ideas)

You can make a huge difference for people you know.

What are you doing to earn more referrals?

• • •

2. Help Others Get What They Want First ...and Then Asking for Referrals Gets a Whole Lot Easier.

> *"You can get everything you want in life if you just help enough other people get what they want."*
>
> —Zig Ziglar

This just might be the most important quotation in the book! I know this has almost become a cliché, but like most clichés it's founded on a great deal of truth. Maybe nobody has ever done any scientific research on it, but it surely seems that the more you give to others, the more you get.

The more you go above and beyond with a client, the more business you get

The more you help a center of influence, the more business comes back to you.

It's not always tit for tat, and you certainly don't want to keep score. You might send three pieces of business to one professional and help someone at a networking event find a job. You might not receive anything specific from these people, but perhaps you'll get all kinds of opportunities from others.

Why do we hear so much about helping others and yet often find it hard to do?

It is counter-intuitive. Research has shown that humans, are innately wired to focus on their own needs 95% of the time. If you're spending 95% of your time focused on getting referrals, that's great. The only problem is that you really need to spend more than 5% of your time thinking about how you can help others. It also means that the people you want referrals from are not thinking about you!

Two years ago, I met an attorney who had brought in $1.1 million of new business for his firm in 2006. He attributed it almost entirely to the fact that he had referred so much business to others. He did a lot of giving and he didn't keep score about who gave back. He just knew that creating that much good will would make good things happen.

You will often have to help others succeed *first*—or at least try. And you'll need to keep helping them. With clients this means continually taking care of their needs as well as you know how and listening for other ways to make an impact. With centers of influence (COI) – other key professionals in your network who have a similar target market - it means a lot more:

Start a new action habit: Schedule time to add value to COIs and key clients. This will start a new mental habit of putting COI needs high on your priority list.

This is not easy to do and for most sales professionals, it does not come naturally. It takes practice and it needs to be drilled into your head.

I don't know how many times I had to hear that before it truly sunk in—I think for me it took about four years. That's how hard it was to get off focusing only on immediate business. The sooner you do it, the better.

I recently asked Adam, an insurance agent and past client of mine, why he was the only agent in his office to have referral partners. Listen for his reasons:

"My first question used to be 'what's in it for me?' 'How can he help me?' I wasn't thinking long term; I was only thinking about myself. I really needed a mindset shift. I had to trust you (as my referral coach) that it would be worth my while. And Tim {a former agent in his office} had had great success getting referrals

from other professionals and he had worked with you so I knew it was possible, and he spoke really highly of you. I had no idea back then how great it could be."

- SIX reasons before he was ready to do something! Now because Adam has done such a good job referring business to other professionals, he is a Presidents Club qualifier in his company, 70% of his business comes from referrals, and 80% of that business comes from COIs.

I took a week off recently and returned to reading one of my favorite authors, Stephen Covey. **This quotation grabbed me by the jugular so much** that I had to read and re-read it several times. It is from his book *First Things First*:

> ***"We settle for the illusion society sells us that meaning is in self-focus – self-esteem, self-improvement. But the wisdom literature of thousands of years repeatedly validates the reality that the greatest fulfillment in improving ourselves comes in our empowerment to more effectively reach out and help others. Quality of life is inside out. Meaning is in contribution, in living for something higher than self."***

Too often I get caught in the trap of thinking too egotistically about 'what can I do that will help me and quick-fix cheer me up?' and **missing the point that I feel best when I'm helping others** grow their business by getting more referrals, when I'm coaching kids improv comedy on a Tuesday night, spending time with friends and family, and/or playing with my sister's children who are five and seven.

This is the kind of paradigm shift that could change everything for you. Happiness is not in the "me, me, me," but in making a difference to others. And that's where the referrals come, too!

• • •

3. Understand and Apply the 'Rule for Reciprocation.'

> *"We should try to repay, in kind, what another person has provided us."*
>
> — Robert Cialdini's *Rule for Reciprocation*

For the past seven years I've listened to audio programs extolling the importance of bringing something to the table, of adding value first. Recently, sales coach and author Bob Burg published a book titled *The Go-Giver,* which shares the compelling message of helping others. The idea is virtually a cliché!

There were times when this drove me nuts as I thought to myself; "I can't spend my time doling out free advice and helping others with their causes—I've got a business to run!" At times it sounded fluffy and new age. I felt like saying; "Yeah, easy for you to say, Mr. Millionaire International Speaker! I've got a growing relationship with my credit card company!" So here's what you need to understand as soon as possible:

The reason why helping other people is so highly recommended is because people feel obligated to return the favor!
Read this again!

Nobody had ever explained this to me before.

I knew deep down it made some sense but taking the leap of faith was difficult for me. Now that I've read the psychology research, it makes sense. Cialdini first wrote about this in *Influence: The Psychology of Persuasion*. He makes it clear that it is innate to humans that we feel we must help someone in return *provided the help they gave us was genuine and unconditional*. (If we sense it's a scheme of sorts, it won't work.)

He notes that when we need to persuade and influence others we mistakenly ask ourselves: "who can help me here?" This approach rarely works because it comes off as needy—rather like saying: "I really need your help growing my business. Can you please please refer me to everyone you know?" No! In Cialdini's latest book called, *YES! 50 Secrets from the Science of Persuasion,* he advises:

> *"We suggest it would be more productive to ask ourselves the question 'whom can I help?', knowing that the norm of reciprocation and the social obligation it confers on others will make future requests more effective."*

This is why it's vital to know what value you've brought to a client before asking them for referrals (*Step 2 of the Six-Step Fearless Referral Conversation, see Chapter* 6). Have you helped them enough to earn a referral?

Also, have boundaries in your business week about who you help and keep in mind that it may be a while before the favor is returned. I hate to sound calculating, but you are growing a business, not a non-profit organization. Absolutely there are times to help others who are reaching out to you; mentoring others is incredibly rewarding. But most people don't have the time or money to randomly help everyone who knocks on their door. Does that person you're helping know others who might make good clients for you?

A friend of mine in the financial services industry developed a huge network and became known as a great resource for helping people between jobs. The problem is that somewhere along the line, people met with her expecting free advice and were not interested in discussing their financial situation with her and potential retirement rollover money. After some time, my friend simply grew resentful at not being appreciated.

Interestingly, this is where I find the universal principle of how much you like the other person makes a big difference!

There are five things to consider if you want a BIG return from helping others:

a) ***"The more a person gives to us, the more obligated we feel to give in return."*** Is your light bulb on now?

b) **A gift or favor is most persuasive.**
Three factors:

i) It needs to be seen by the recipient as significant or meaningful.

A financial advisor friend of mine was telling me recently that she was disappointed by the lack of response she had gotten from subscribing some of her clients to *National Geographic*. She had wanted to send something of value that both spouses might like. Unfortunately, the magazine evidently did not mean enough to those who got it. That's because:

ii) It needs to be personalized.

What are you most interested in? What would you remove from your mailbox and say: "This is cool!"? What are your primary needs right now?

I was in England last summer speaking to an organization about networking. Afterwards, someone told me about some business that took four years to come her way. But during that time she had met the needs of her prospect several times by recommending writers to her (which was her prospect's primary need during this period).

iii) Unexpected is best

This supports research done by Harvard psychologist Daniel Gilbert and by GALLUP. I cannot recommend this idea more highly. I have had tremendous success surprising people with small gifts. Remember: it has to be sincere!

Last year, on two different occasions, sales managers who had brought me in to present to their teams stood up during this point in my seminar and explained to their salespeople that they had decided to select me after unexpectedly receiving a book from me.

Who's a big prospect of yours? What could you do that would be a happy surprise for them?

• • •

4. Make Emotional Bank Account Deposits.

> *"Today the customer wants a relationship before deciding on your offer. In fact, the customer will choose a better relationship over a better price. The relationship today between you and the customer is the key element in the decision. People today only buy from people they like."*
>
> — Brian Tracy

One of the fundamental principles to getting referrals is you can't get water out of an empty well. You can't ask for anything if you haven't been adding value, making "deposits" and filling up the well yourself first. You wouldn't readily recommend anything if it hadn't really done anything good for you. Your integrity is on the line.

Stephen Covey coined the phrase "emotional bank account." His concept was that you can't have a strong relationship without constantly feeding it positive "deposits." When you are adding to it on a regular basis, then there can be some give and take. If you ignore building it the right way, you can't expect anything in return. The same is true for referrals.

The last time I bought a new car, I got a call from the company asking me if I would recommend the dealership to friends and family. Over the phone I said I would because my experience had been very positive. But after I hung up, I concluded that I would hesitate to refer them. I was trying to understand why I wouldn't recommend them. I thought about it and realized that the car had to deliver for a while. I've had some bad experiences with cars, and I realized that I wouldn't recommend one until I knew it was coming through for me.

So far one good deposit has been made, but in this instance I will need many more before I would suggest someone else go there. For example, the salesperson who helped me didn't really seem very interested in me and what I did for a living (which strikes me as really strange since he could have fished for some free advice!). He earned the referral on his competence, but he did little to build the relationship.

I remember meeting someone at a business happy hour once. I barely spoke to him, didn't connect with him on a personal level when we did talk, and then was amazed when he started leaving me messages asking me to introduce his wife (whom I'd never met) to all my contacts in a specific industry! No "deposits" had been made and yet he was asking me to risk my reputation for a total stranger. It's an extreme example, but it reminds us we need to track the balance of lifting or leaning on a relationship.

How You Can Apply This Knowledge To Get More Referrals.

1. **Have Value Conversations with your clients.**
   This is discussed in detail in Chapter 6. Helping clients to realize fully how much you have helped them and ***acknowledge what you have done for them recently*** solidifies part one of the Rule for Reciprocation. You will hear whether you have made enough deposits and have earned the referral. IF your client tells you that you have brought value, it makes transitioning to what you and I call a referral conversation that much easier.

2. **Keep regularly adding value to clients, referral partners, and potential centers of influence without expecting any immediate return.**
   This is something you can do every week. And you should do regularly, so your top 20% of contacts know that you have done something for them recently! Please: schedule it now! Make it a regular habit in your business week. Then the only question you need to answer is: How can I most add value to this person?

3. **Send items of value to your client base to keep top of mind.**
   This could include free helpful information that is not selling them something and that they might actually want to read—not pitch in the recycling bin. Perhaps articles or books on topics that interest them, such as antique cars, hiking or other hobbies would be appreciated.

4. **Hold a client appreciation event.**
   There are so many variations and possibilities here that can benefit the rule for reciprocation.

5. **Send luxury gifts at holiday time.**
   My friend Curt runs a software company, and he sends out high-quality wines, cigars, and chocolates during the holidays that are highly ap-

preciated by his clients. He always has new business pouring in—not just in January.

Be aware that some companies cannot accept gifts for fear it be perceived as a kick-back from a vendor. It is important people do not feel you are taking advantage of them.

Master #2, 3, and 4 because these are the founding principles that govern the relationships you need to get a lot of referrals.

• • •

5. First Be Competent and Jargon-free

> *"Accumulate enough knowledge that you can share it with others—so you can enable them to profit from your knowledge as much as you do... it's important, it's powerful, it's essential. Thus it is value currency."*
>
> — Tim Sanders, *Love is the Killer App*

Often I like to ask audiences about whom they have referred business to. I ask them to think about the qualities of the people they recommend to loved ones. There are only about five or six qualities that come up consistently. Competence is always one of them.

Nobody will recommend you if they think you are shaky on your subject matter.

This is the first area you must be strong in as quickly as possible. There's a reason why every book on success talks about being a lifelong learner. Knowledge builds trust. As I write this today, I have just come from doing two presentations that were attended by just over 5% of the association's invited membership. 5%. Few people are committed to continuous self-improvement, yet that's exactly what our clients want from us and that's exactly what will help you avoid being downsized.

I cannot say that the best informed person always runs the strongest business. It's not the only skill. Knowledge is only meaningful when you use it. But I can say that your knowledge base can only help you AND lack of competence will hurt you and damage your credibility and authenticity.

How do you handle this if you're new to your profession? Three things: a) write down all the questions you're getting and position yourself as someone who is a learner, who is always taking time to develop professionally, and has access to the information; b) schedule time every day to learn new content and never drop this habit; c) Inform your prospects about your learning habits and goals and any classes/certifications in the works. This IS powerful because everyone knows how rare this is regardless of your age or experience.

Interestingly, I have heard too many times for me to disbelieve that are instances when some of your clients will respect you *more* when you tell them not to expect you to have all the answers. We can't pretend to know everything and certainly should not pretend to know something we don't.

Clearly this depends on your field to some extent. For example, I expect my dentist to know how to fix one of my teeth; I can't expect him to predict to the exact month how long the repair work he has done will last (especially given my sweet tooth!).

A client of mine was telling me about some work she had done on her basement. While there had been a contract for some initial work done, she had trusted her contractor enough to continue on with a second stage of work that needed doing without anything formal in writing. It turns out that this contractor had never done this kind of work before but did not tell her.

Instead my client experienced an endless period of non-deadlines, broken verbal commitments, and unreturned calls and emails because he was trying to figure out how to do the work without admitting it! Needless to say, the frustration levels ran very high.

Even though this person was well liked by my client, this experience built up distrust. She recently told me that she could never recommend this contractor to anyone else.

Here's what I recommend: Develop the habit of reading something from your field at least three times per week for 30 minutes. First thing in the morning is usually the best time. Always be on the lookout for what Tim Sanders calls the book's Big Thought (which he suggests making a drawing of—I need to try that) so you can explain it clearly to someone else. It never ceases to amaze me how quickly I work in that new knowledge when talking with clients or presenting to groups. The ideas seem to sit there like freshly cooked meals waiting a few moments before being passed out by the wait staff at a busy restaurant and devoured by an appreciative audience.

I was travelling through Philadelphia recently and I met a consultant named Joe Sharkey who works all over the USA for a telecommunications company based in Utah. Thirty years ago Joe trained as an engineer, so he knew all the technical aspects to his business. But it was only when he started helping the sales team of his company, that he learned how to avoid technical jargon. "The bankers I meet with often tell me that I do a really good job explaining things in language they can understand."

Joe does such a good job explaining everything that now when he meets with investment bankers, his client will invite peers so they can hear his expertise. His delivery is so compelling that they call him with referrals – although it did take him quite a few years to get to this point! So once you know your stuff, do your best to make sure that your clients truly understand everything you are saying.

In their book *Storyselling for Financial Advisors,* authors Scott West and Mitch Anthony argue that many clients walk away from meetings with advisors feeling confused. The fear some salespeople have is that they are going to come across as unintelligent or average by speaking exclusively in layman's terms. Your clients do not want to feel foolish and may be wary of asking too many questions. Ask yourself if you might be using jargon as a crutch because you have not found a more effective way to communicate.

"Of course you are a professional. So are doctors and lawyers, but we still prefer the ones who can come down off their eight-syllable soapbox and speak to us in a way that illuminates rather than confounds."

• • •

6. Exceed Your Customer and Employee Expectations By 1%

It costs five times more to get a new client than to retain one.

— Phillip Kotler, *Kotler on Marketing*

"Recognizing experiences as a distinct economic offering provides the key to future economic growth...to figure out how to better engage clients to turn the service into a memorable event."

— B. Joseph Pine & James H. Gilmore

You can't expect referrals if your service is simply what your client expects (average). That may sound totally obvious but the next two points are not.

There are two BIG problems with doing what you may well be doing now:

1. I hear quite a lot from certain people about their customer satisfaction surveys and how well they have performed on them. Yet these people also get very few referrals. **Aiming simply for customer satisfaction is no longer adequate** – for retention or referrals!

   In their book *Raving Fans,* Ken Blanchard and Sheldon Bowles state that satisfied customers are satisfied SHEEP "*just parked on your doorstep until something better comes along*." You have to do more than that to keep your clients as repeat business and have them endorse you to others.

   Sales guru Jeffrey Gitomer makes an amusing point about what's most important: Would you rather have your spouse be loyal or would you settle for your spouse just being satisfied?!

2. *Almost all* **business people think their customer service is what sets them apart!**
   Please stop and think about this for a moment. How many times have you heard another professional say that's what makes his or her business better than the competition is customer service? This can't be. So be brutally honest with yourself and ask: Is what I do really any different or better? How is it truly better? I suspect that often we tell ourselves that simply because WE show up, it has to be better. That's like saying the Audubon Society should put each of us on the endangered species list because there's only one of us!

   Ask yourself: What are the key skill areas you need to be strong in and how do you compare to your competition? If you're not sure, survey your clients. At least interview a few of them.

Blanchard and Bowles argue that **"wow" customer service is not a sustainable practice.** If someone comes into an insurance agent's office to make a monthly payment on their car insurance, is it fair to expect the agent to send flowers or a gift certificate in the mail for a steakhouse? That would be absurd.

They argue that we should strive to meet expectations plus 1%. It's going the extra inch. That's an achievable practice that develops even better service over time and creates what they call raving fans. After all, it's the little things that make a difference, right?

It is worth pausing to ask: How can I improve the service my clients get?

In *The Experience Economy,* B. Joseph Pine and James Gilmore make a great case for sprucing up your office or workplace environment and making it a more pleasurable experience—"a memorable event." They coin phrases and write about environments that offer "eatertainment" and "shoppertainment." This can include anything from classical music (apparently this makes you feel more grand so you spend more grand!) and flowers to works of art/photography and great tasting (and smelling) coffee. Banks and car dealerships are getting in on this act with fireplaces, comfortable seating, fresh-baked cookies, community notice boards, children's artwork—and it does make a difference and appeal to the senses.

A couple of years ago I did a workshop in Massachusetts for a financial advisor and his referral group, which consisted of influential professionals in his community. When I saw his office, he had it all: an electronic sign with the names of clients coming in that day, classical music playing in the background, china cups and quality coffee, muffins and cookies in a basket, unique artwork and interesting framed pictures, sports memorabilia signed by well-known coaches and athletes from the Red Sox, Celtics, and Patriots, a broad choice of current magazines, and an elaborate aquarium. He also had a high-end follow-up system for once a client had visited. There is likely more that I have forgotten. It was remarkable; it made me feel classy and appreciated. And anyone can start this process. He had been in business for 25 years and he had implemented many ideas he'd learned from conferences over the years.

Despite the wealth of knowledge available today about best business practices, isn't it bizarre that most of us have LOW expectations as customers? To develop raving fans, Blanchard and Bowles recommend that you:

1. **Decide what you want.** Create a vision of your business and draw boundaries: you can't be all things to all people! What would you like to spend more time specializing in? Who are your favorite clients and do they make up a certain demographic?
2. **Find out what your clients want.** (their vision). Does it fit with yours? Use their ideas to help you BUT keep these ideas in line with what YOU do best. Remember: they will not have the big picture that you have, only specific hot buttons.
3. **Deliver the vision—plus 1%.** It's not about under-promising and over-delivering; it's about consistently meeting expectations and then doing just a little bit more. People do notice whether you follow-up promptly or not and when you say you will (one reason they do notice is because most people do not keep their word on what they

say they will do and we remember!). It is always one of the five or six things that come up when I ask people why they refer others.

Charles Walgreen, the founder of the Walgreens pharmacy, described success including customer service as: *"Doing a thousand little things the right way—doing many of them over and over again."*

Don't forget about your employees!

According to Gallup's Peter Flade, having emotionally engaged employees is as important as having happy customers. How come nobody seems to talk about this?

A great example of this was learned thirty years ago by Sam Walton whose employees had a poor reputation for how well they were treating customers. What he learned was that if his managers treated his employees well, the happy employees would then be nicer to the customers who would then have a positive shopping experience. He noted; *"the customers will return again and again, and that is where the real profit in this business lies."* It was an innovative way to gauge customer satisfaction that proved very effective. And it all started at the top.

Advantages also include employees who are more productive, stay with your company longer, are absent less, and have a better safety record. All of which also means lower training and replacement expenses for you.

Sean, one of the sales managers I currently coach to get referrals for recruiting prospects, has started taking one of his reps out for lunch each week. It has been a huge success. He asks them to block out two hours. The bulk of the meeting (and the primary goal) is focused on how they are doing and how he can help them improve in their business.

He takes on the role of coach, so he offers specific positive feedback, support, accountability, and direction on what they are not seeing about their performance. The atmosphere is more relaxed and conducive to more open dialogue, which means making an emotional connection away from the hustle of the office, the multiple phone calls and sales appointments. It's a distraction-free environment (unless the wait staff is cute!) where it is easier to show that he truly cares.

And there is a win for Sean. His reps are expected to come with three referrals for him (he aims high and they average one quality referral each time). The win for the reps is that they can take on a leadership role in helping the person they recommend succeed because they know they are bringing that person onto a winning team. Sean has created his own additional rewards as well after asking his reps what else would motivate them.

Strong customer (and employee) service is a must in order to earn the right to ask for referrals and to expect them.

"The new economy is described by some commentators as a relationship economy. Why? Because customers don't just want a great price or a fast delivery, they also want a good experience."

— Robert Holden

"The best things in life are not things."

— Anonymous

• • •

7. Why Loyalty Matters Most

*"**Emotionally satisfied customers contribute far more to the bottom line** than rationally satisfied customers do, even though they are equally 'satisfied'"*

— *Gallup*

When I need to go to my bank, I have several branches to choose from. But there's only one that I can honestly say I look forward to visiting, where it doesn't feel like a chore that's out of my way.

That's the one where there are two tellers who seem genuinely interested in what I am doing and what's going on in my life. I really enjoy talking to them and they have a good sense of humor. They even ask about my dating life (umm: that might be book number three or four perhaps!). It doesn't have to get more complicated than that. When I was then introduced to a different banker that trusted people in my network spoke highly about, I just couldn't get interested because I really like the people I see at my current financial institution. They care about me and they're happy to see me.

You already intellectually know that connecting with people on an emotional level is more powerful than simply meeting their expectations. My challenge to you is to stop and think about how well connected you are to your clients. Do they know the real you? How often do you laugh together? Have you ever shared why you do what you do? This can be a compelling story that demonstrates how much you care. And I don't want to just suggest that you have to be drinking buddies to make an emotional connection (although it doesn't hurt!). Nor do you have to be especially personable to get results.

The power of increased client loyalty: In Frederick Reichheld's *The Loyalty Effect,* he argues that by retaining the right clients—those in the top 20%—and developing 5% more of these into loyal customers, you can increase your profits from 25% to 100%! Being referred to these individuals is the most effective way to make this happen. So how do you it?

First, recognize the challenges with developing a loyal client base.

Here are six of the challenges identified in the work of Keiningham, Vavra, Aksoy, and Wallard in *Loyalty Myths:*

- Attracting and retaining clients are BOTH critical processes.
- Client loyalty must be consistently earned.
- **Loyal clients do not generally talk about your business** (remember 20-60-20?)
- Most companies keep terrible records of their clients.

- There is no consistent relationship between employee satisfaction, customer satisfaction, and business productivity.
- In a competitive marketplace, offers and actions that once delighted clients are now expected.

Three solutions to help you develop a loyal client base come from research done at Gallup by Alec Applebaum.

- First, managers should instill in their staff a belief and understanding that their products/services are as flawless as possible. This goes back to the beliefs we all must have before we can ask for referrals. When the belief is there, the confidence builds and the loyalty develops.

- Second, managers should train their employees to act as ambassadors of the brand because that indicates a loyal culture. For example, this could include having one of the assistants in the office saying to a prospect: "You're really going to enjoy meeting with Christine. She does such a good job. Her clients just love her, and those of us in the office think she is wonderful to work with."

"Every and any interaction with a customer—such as a new sales opportunity or complaint handling—is a chance to develop a relationship and build an emotional connection."

— Peter Flade, *Gallup Organization, UK.*

- Third, client problems should be transformed into opportunities to please clients. I know the word "transform" gets overused in marketing. However, when a client gets over his or her initial emotional reaction and accepts that you are a human being that erred, you can turn things around most of the time. One of our challenges is that we hate to admit we were wrong or made a mistake. Be a grown-up! That is where you start. Then you right the wrongs and show you truly care and exceed their expectations by 1%. If you are being sincere, you will build loyalty.

> *"Staging experiences is not about entertaining customers; it is about engaging them."*
>
> — Pine and Gilmore

DO IT! Think about this one in the car and then act on your best ideas one at a time: How can you engage your clients on a more emotional level?

CHAPTER 3:

Becoming Fearless

1. Face Your Fear of Rejection and Fear of People

While most of us hate to admit it, let's come clean about our #1 challenge. Most people in sales are, at best, uncomfortable contacting strangers and uncomfortable meeting them. At worst, they can't even pick up the phone because they're afraid of the responses they might get and that their feelings might get hurt.

The same is often true when asking for referrals. The vast majority of people are not comfortable doing it. I see it as the number one obstacle for most people.

You don't need a Ph.D. in psychology to know that the solution is to face your fears. It's not easy. If it were easy, everyone would make many more sales and the turnover in your industry would be much, much lower.

Brian Tracy gives the perfect example when he suggests that you imagine that you have been given a long list of people who all want to buy what you sell, but you only have until midnight to contact them. He asks, "What time would you start that day? How late would you work? Would you find other things to do before making your calls? Would you take coffee breaks? Would you take an hour for lunch? No! You would be contacting as many people as possible! There would no hesitation!"

What matters is that:

1. **You admit to yourself the truth and not blame other things,** such as not having a polished referral script, elevator speech, or high-end sales materials to hand out.

2. **You get enough leverage on yourself to face your fears.** This is based on what I covered in Chapter 1: you act either when the pain gets too great or the pleasure juices you up enough to be driven to take more action. That's your responsibility.

 Here are some ideas that help from marketing expert Robert Middleton:

 a) **Most people are also afraid of you and that you will judge and reject them!** It's time to start noticing that most people avoid your eye contact in public and avoid interacting with you. Frankly, it is unbelievable! Be more aware of this fear that others have and make a mental shift—use this knowledge to empower yourself. Say to yourself, "They might be uncomfortable too; I should put their mind at ease. I am not a shark. If they're interested, great, I can help them. And if they're not interested, it's okay—not everyone is going to be interested."

 b) **Stop listening to the bad advice of a young child.** As children, almost all of us experience some emotionally painful rejection and make some strong reactive decisions (often at a very young age) that we never want to experience that rejection again. The challenge is that we are still listening to this young child's bad advice. Why would you do this? This (let's say) 6 year-old is saying, "Be afraid of everyone because they might hurt your feelings!!!" Would you only listen to the advice of a 6-year-old on other life decisions?

 c) **Focus on the other person:** The founder of Mary Kay Cosmetics had a great saying that everyone has an invisible sign around their neck that says: "Make me feel important." Yes, it's a smart way to treat someone; yes, it also reduces their fears, but most importantly, it gets your focus off yourself and onto something constructive. Your fears will be reduced.

 d) **How you look at any situation in life is a CHOICE!** Every way you interpret a situation can be looked at in a completely different way. There are people who go through a relationship break up and are empowered to finally be free of something negative; other people are devastated and vow never to be hurt so much again (only recently did I realize I had done that one to myself). There are salespeople out there who truly enjoy doing the things that make others uncomfortable. As Stephen Covey says: "If you want to change your life, you've got to change your paradigms."

How would you promote yourself if you knew you couldn't fail?

e) **Use a little inspiration to remind yourself that you are never alone:**

"The brave man is not he who does not feel afraid but he who conquers fear."

— Nelson Mandela

"Courage is rightly considered the foremost of virtues, for upon it, all others depend."

— Winston Churchill

"We need to be able to charge headlong into the inferno of our most horrific fears..that takes courage, and that's why courage is a prerequisite for happiness."

— Dan Baker, *What Happy People Know*

"Success is letting go of fear."

— Carl Whittaker, World Games gold medal winner

"Sometimes our worst fears are like dragons guarding our deepest treasure."

— Rainer Maria Rilke, Austrian poet

• • •

2. Face It Some More!

What's the #1 need almost every business owner and salesperson has? More prospects, right?

Fear of rejection is so often the main obstacle to contacting and meeting more prospects. The solution is to face your fears more and more by building your "courage muscle." I know from my own experience that this is much easier said than done.

Courage, a book written by British Prime Minister Gordon Brown, does a magnificent job of putting our day-to-day fears into perspective. Where do your fears stand in the grand scheme of things?

I truly hope that these three incredible stories help you face your fears better and see them in a truer perspective.

Raoul Wallenberg.

This Swedish banker had a very comfortable life in a neutral country during World War Two. Even though he wasn't Jewish himself, he was so outraged by what the Nazis were doing that he chose to go to Hungary, one of the world's most chaotic and unsafe places in July 1944, to save as many Jews as he could from extermination. His accomplishments are remarkable.

Want Courage? When Jews were being rounded up to be taken to the death camps, he would calmly walk up to the SS commander and tell him he had Swedish protection passes and that if any Jews were taken away this commander would be reported and hanged as a war criminal. He saved as many as 25,000 Jews this way even though he forged many of the passes. 25,000! One eyewitness recalled:

"He stood out there in the street, probably feeling the loneliest man in the world, trying to pretend that there was something behind him. They could have shot him there and then in the street and nobody would have known about it."

On another occasion, he actually invited Adolf Eichmann, head of operations for Hitler's Final Solution, over for dinner. Eichmann was obsessed with wiping Jews out of existence. Yet Wallenberg told him that the Nazis were going to lose the war and then he explained why Nazi ideology was so flawed! Eichmann was so enraged by this that he told Wallenberg: "Accidents do happen, even to a neutral diplomat."

Wallenberg disappeared once the Soviets arrived and is believed to have died in one of their Gulag camps, aged 33.

Would you have the courage to do this knowing you would likely never see your home country and family again? Is it really so uncomfortable to ask for that referral when you've helped someone out?

Martin Luther King, Jr.

Picture this: It's January 1956. Your newborn is asleep in her cot and your young spouse is fast asleep too. But your house was recently fire-bombed and you've had numerous death threats. It's after midnight and you're sitting alone at the kitchen table with a cold cup of coffee. You've just received another phone call telling you to get out of town before you or your wife and child will be killed. What would you do?

It was at this point that Martin Luther King found his courage had deserted him. He was terrified and had a panicked conversation with God. "I tried to think of a way to move out of the picture without appearing a coward. I got to the point that I couldn't take it any longer. I was weak."

Was a seat on a city bus worth putting his family at risk for?

As he prayed, "the quiet assurance of an inner voice saying, 'Martin Luther, stand up for righteousness. Stand up for justice. Stand up for truth.' At that moment I experienced the presence of the Divine as I had never experienced Him before. Almost at once my fears began to go."

King was assassinated twelve years later in 1968 aged 39.

I understand that the cause of our livelihood is likely not as jugular as King's. But if King faced death threats for over a decade, how long do you think it would take for you to get past your prospecting fears if you faced them every day with the same amount of courage? Everyone concurs that our fear diminishes when we confront it over and over.

Aung San Suu Kyi

She is the world's most renowned female prisoner of conscience. While living a very comfortable life in England as a wife of an Oxford professor and a mother, she returned to her home country, Burma, in 1988 as prodemocracy movements swept the country.

Her father had secured independence for Burma from the British in 1947, but he was assassinated that same year. So she decided to fulfill her duty to a father and country she loved.

Despite preaching non-violent protest and despite being democratically elected in 1990 to be prime minister (with 81% of the votes!), she has been under house arrest without charge since July 1989—more than 20 years! Courage? Her arrest came on a day when she and some of her colleagues confronted an army unit who were pointing their guns at her. Rather than surrender, she walked at them alone offering herself as an easy target.

Her best-known writings are called *Freedom From Fear*; can you apply this to your business?

> *"Fearlessness may be a gift, but perhaps more precious is the courage acquired through endeavor; courage that comes from cultivating the habit of refusing to let fear dictate one's actions, courage that could be described as "grace under pressure"—grace which is renewed repeatedly in the face of harsh, unremitting pressure."*

Aung San Suu Kyi won the Nobel Peace Prize in 1991. In May 2008, after Cyclone Nargis hit Burma, Suu Kyi lost her roof and was living in virtual darkness after she lost electricity in her dilapidated lakeside bungalow. She is now 65 years old and has rarely been allowed to see her two children since 1988. She has always had the option to leave Burma and live in comfort, but she has refused since she would never be allowed to return and fight for democracy.

Got the courage to sustain your beliefs about what's right for 20 years despite confined to your decaying house by a paranoid military dictatorship? How long have you been uncomfortable about asking for referrals? Do you have it in you to push through this? How long might that take?

Courage: Three middle-class professionals who could all have chosen a quiet, comfortable life and never become well known. They all learned how to find more courage. You are not being asked to put your life on the line or your family's safety at stake. What do you want out of your life? Is it time to hold your chin up higher and say, "I'm not walking into a life-threatening situation. I am extending my help to others. I believe in what I'm doing. If they don't want it, that's their loss. I will move on and show more courage. If it was easy, everyone would do it. I intend to do it."

As humans we are all made of the same stuff. What are you made of and how much of this is showing?

• • •

3. Overcome the Biggest Myth in Our Culture

Some time ago, I was invited to the annual awards banquet of an international financial services company. When the top producer for the year walked up to the podium to "say a few words," I was not expecting anything earth-shattering. What he said was amazing and inspiring. First he told his life story with such passion that it took my breath away. He was a former teacher (like myself) who now absolutely loved what he did. He was living his mission, not working a job.

Then he asked those in the audience who were in their first five years in the industry to stand up. I expected a motivational plug to them, but instead he looked them in the eye and explained how they would never know how many times he had felt like a failure. He shared that he almost quit on numerous occasions in his early years, and that he even kept his teaching license current just in case. Most highly accomplished people have fallen on their faces many times but they keep getting up.

Here are three priceless observations on "failure":

1) Relationship expert Barbara DeAngelis points out that *"The only path to success is to do it badly first."*

2) Billionaire rebel Richard Branson once said of his accomplishments, *"I've just failed a lot more than most people."*

3) *Success Intelligence* author Robert Holden states that **most people define "successful people" as "people who have not failed at anything."** Clearly, it's a huge myth in our culture that high-achieving people were all overnight sensations, that getting to the top was pretty seamless and their success is because of innate talent.

   On the contrary, there have been many well-known people who have had all kinds of rejections and failures but have become successful *"because they have used their failures well."* Here are a few classic examples from Holden's book:

"As a composer, he is hopeless."
— A music teacher referring to one of his students, Ludwig van Beethoven

"He has no talent at all, that boy...Tell him please to give up painting."
— Edouart Manet to Claude Monet, 1864.

"He is too stupid to learn anything and should think of a career where he might succeed by virtue of his pleasant personality."
— A teacher writing about his student, Thomas Edison.

"Can't act. Can't Sing. Balding. Can dance a little."
— MGM executive on a screen test by an aspiring entertainer called Fred Astaire, 1928.

"He lacked imagination and had no good ideas."
— Newspaper editor after firing his employee, Walt Disney.

"You'd better learn secretarial work or else get married."

— Director of Blue Book Modeling Agency to would-be actress Marilyn Monroe, 1944

"You ought to go back to drivin' a truck."

— The theatre manager who fired a singer called Elvis Presley after one performance, 1954

"We don't think your ideas have any merit here."

— IBM executive to a young man named Bill Gates

"You'll never make any money out of children's books."

— The publisher who took on JK Rowling's first Harry Potter book. (Rowling is now the highest earning woman in England at over $400,000,000.)

So what can you do to achieve your dream of being a high achiever?

1. **Realize that falling on your face is normal.**
2. **Develop a support system.**

The high achiever who spoke at the event said he could not have done what he's done without the unconditional support of his spouse. He went on further to say that without a supportive spouse you could not fulfill your potential. Napoleon Hill cited a great support system as one of his four "musts" to think and grow rich (in all areas of life).

What is your support system? You can get creative about this (beyond people). It can include anything empowering that makes you feel good: audio programs, books, photos, inspiring music and literature, pets, or even locations. Build a support team around you (*see Chapter 7 for more on this*). I believe it also means minimizing time with energy vampires—negative people. You become the sum of the five people you spend the most time with. Tony Robbins is most succinct on this: "*Who you spend time with is who you become.*"

3. **Build empowering beliefs about yourself**

See the last section of this chapter: Become Your #1 Fan.

4. **Define success and failure for yourself.**

You decide your own definition of success. For example, "I did my best and learned something." You decide when you deserve to feel like a failure. This might be when you have not kept your word or perhaps haven't lived according to your values. This is infinitely superior to feeling badly because your house isn't as large as someone else's or that someone makes more money than you.

The ultimate belief is to accept that 'failure' is only a necessary and normal part of the journey.

• • •

4. Stop Making Excuses

> *"A man can get discouraged many times, but he is not a failure until he begins to blame somebody else and stop trying."*
>
> — John Burroughs, Writer

How much responsibility do you really take—for your life and your referral business?

On a scale of 1-10 how much responsibility do you take for everything in your life? I think this is an area where we fool ourselves.

Who is responsible?

Who do you suppose said this? *"I have spent the best years of my life giving people the lighter pleasures—helping them have a good time. And all I get is abuse: the existence of a hunted man."*

Are you any closer on the above quotation? It was Al Capone. I spent an entire semester of college in 1989 doing a U.S. history independent study on Capone and organized crime in Chicago in the 1920's. Without going into detail, he either killed personally or sentenced dozens of people to premature and violent death.

I was revisiting Dale Carnegie's *How to Win Friends and Influence People.* I wish I had listened to my own advice on repeatedly listening to good material when it came to this. It's full of so much common sense that I overlooked its incredible value the last time I read it. I failed to ask myself enough: "How well am I applying this in my own life?" This is simple yet priceless content that will make a huge impact on your personal AND business life.

Carnegie tells another story from the 1930's of a man in a car who was kissing his girlfriend and got interrupted by a police officer asking to see his driver's license. The man responded by shooting the officer multiple times before getting out of the car, taking the officer's gun as he lay on the ground dying and then shooting him some more. As he went to the electric chair for this murder, he complained loudly that his sentence was unjust: "I was only defending myself."

I was floored. How could someone not take such responsibility I asked myself? Still wondering if it was possible, I picked up that day's local newspaper. The headline story was about a 23 year-old woman who had killed her youngest child. Her reason? "I only have enough love for one child," she explained. Slowly my years of teaching middle school came back to me and I began to recall all the feeble excuses I heard from students about not doing homework. "Who's responsible for doing your work?" I would ask, and there would usually be an awkward silence followed by a quiet "I am." Did it make difference? I failed more students than any other teacher—and I do not miss the stress that caused!

The Responsibility Scale

Three years ago I went to a Brian Tracy seminar. During the first break I went up to talk to him. I guess I really didn't think through what I wanted to ask him. I just wanted to talk to him in person. He had been telling his remarkable life story for 90 minutes and weaving in what it took to be successful. All I could muster was a vague: "Your story is amazing. How did you do it?" He looked slightly exasperated as if to say, "Weren't you listening to anything I just said?"

Then he thought for a moment and told me about how he had been so poor in his early 20's that he would save money on cooking by heating his can of beans on the radiator overnight. **Then one day as he looked**

around his bleak living space, he realized that he had no one else to blame but himself. It was no longer legitimate to blame parents or teachers. Everything he had in life was up to him.

Then he said to me, "If I had to just pinpoint one thing, **I think we all have a responsibility scale inside us. And most people are probably at about a 6. And what I've learned is that you have to move yourself to a 10, take complete ownership of every area of your life, and refuse to blame anyone or anything else."**

Who's responsible for your results? Your health? Your relationships? Your inner peace? Your income?

If you don't like the results you're getting, look at your actions. In many respects, this is two things: a tough pill to swallow for most people and also, very exciting – it's very empowering.

How Much Responsibility Do You Take for Your Referral Business?

1. **Do you forget to ask?**
   This is excuse #1. You have to take responsibility for how you're getting in your own way, for your limiting beliefs and for your courage.

   Do a mini-interview with others and ask them what they think your strengths are and ask them how they think you're getting in your own way.

2. **Do you still forget to ask?**
   Start using meeting agendas and putting something non-threatening on them like "value discussion" instead of "introductions" from which you can pivot to other people your client would like to help by recommending you. (*More on agendas in Chapter 5.*)

3. **Do you ever take "I can't think of anyone" for an answer?**
   Everybody knows 200 people or more. Provided your client talks about the value you have brought (and actually gets specific—not just a nod of the head), it is YOUR job to help your client think of

someone. Most people like to help others. Ask better questions that help jog their memories. Show more confidence in yourself and that you can help people your clients care about. Never accept it when someone suggests you contact others but do not use their name. Find out why or pursue a better referral. (*For more on this, see Chapter 6.*)

4. **Do you have a script?** If you are have no concerns about asking, have you developed wording that works for you?

5. **Do you plant the seeds about referrals with an expectations discussion?** (*See Chapter 5 for that.*)

6. **How well do you narrow down referral requests** so that two to three people come to mind when you ask? (*Chapter 6*)

7. **Educate clients?** Have you developed materials or wording to educate your clients on what a quality referral for you would be? (*Chapter 6*)

8. **Reassure clients.** How well do you reassure your clients about how you follow-up and how you don't expect them to know for sure whether the people they recommend have a need for what you do? (*Chapter 6*)

9. **Coach your clients.** Do you coach your clients on what to say to the people they recommend – most of them have no idea what to say! It's your job to do this. (*Chapter 6*)

10. **Keep control of the referral process.** Do you make sure you always have the next step in the referral process so that you can keep control? (*Chapter 6*)

11. **Have a great follow-up system...and use it.** Do you have a follow up system in place so you don't drop the ball on names you do receive and have a means to thank your referral sources? (*Chapter 7*)

12. **Develop and utilize "Centers of Influence."** Have you developed four to five great centers of influence as referral sources? (See my second book for that topic!)

13. **Plan ahead.** Do you plan your weeks ahead of time to proactively schedule time to do these things? (*Chapter* 7)

Be your own role model:

Since there may not be anyone in your office who can serve as a great role model, take 100% responsibility for your referral business.

If you're not happy with your referral business, only you can do something about it. No quick fix leads program is going to transform your financial situation.

You can access this business. It's just that you may not know anyone in your company to get good guidance on this. It may also be true that there is someone in your office who has a unique way of getting referrals that does not work for others.

Use this book as your solution to get referrals your way. You are responsible for developing a system that works for you because there is no one-size fits all when it comes to getting referrals.

See what I mean? Getting to a 10 on the responsibility scale is not easy! We don't like to admit we've made a mistake, done something wrong, or not taken complete responsibility. What we blame is in our self-talk and the excuses we give to others. Hopefully this will increase your own self-awareness and help you move toward that 10.

• • •

5. Recognize Your Obstacles

> *"The one obstacle that holds you back is the way you see yourself."*
>
> — Fiona Harrold, *Be Your Own Life Coach*

Why don't we take action after coming across a great idea?

About three years ago I went to a Wealth Expo in Chicago featuring Donald Trump and Robert Kiyosaki and was fortunate enough to see Tony Robbins there. He had 9000 people jumping up and down, cheering loudly, and running up and hugging total strangers. I—yes, Mr. Reserved Englishman—was one of them. It sounds really far-fetched, but I know that some of you reading this have had the same experience somewhere.

He pointed out that most people would do nothing with his "life-changing" information. He told everyone to take notes so they would remember what he had talked about. I looked around closely: maybe one in 20 attendees heeded his advice. Let me be clear: I was impressed that day. He hit on numerous jugular issues.

But the other remarkable part was how quickly the energy level changed the minute it was over. As I walked out in this flood of 9000, I could hear conversations on either side of me. Nobody was talking about what they were going to do next to improve their lives. All I could hear were people saying "Yes it was good, but," and finding a flaw in one of Robbins' points and reasons why his seminar had not "worked" for them. Once I left that auditorium, the atmosphere could not have been more different. There was nothing positive or inspiring about it: it was a feeding frenzy of get-rich-quick schemes and sales sharks.

So why is it that 98% of people do nothing after hearing a great idea—including after reading a book?

I asked an audience of financial advisors this question a couple of years ago at the start of one of my referral seminars. Here were their reasons as to why they had taken no action in the past after a great seminar:

- I was too busy
- There were too many good ideas; I didn't know where to start
- I forgot to revisit the material
- I felt there were no new ideas
- I procrastinated
- I didn't fully trust the presenter
- I didn't believe I could do it
- I didn't believe the material would work for me
- I was unwilling to change
- The presenter was there to sell us their program, their books and DVDs
- Past failures: I had tried something new after a seminar in the past and it didn't work
- I didn't make habits out of the new ideas
- Lack of commitment
- Complacent – I felt like I knew it already
- I didn't put the systems in place
- **Fear**

Here Are a Few More Reasons I've Discovered:

a) Deep down, you don't believe you deserve to do better (self-worth).
b) You don't believe in what you are doing for a living.
c) You don't take complete responsibility—you blame someone else for what's not working.
d) You have a scarcity mindset about what's available in life.
e) You are afraid to outshine certain key people in your life.
f) **You need to hear it 10 to 30 times before the light goes on.** As Tony Robbins says; *"Repetition is the mother of success."*
g) You overestimate your uniqueness ("my situation is different") and often refuse to use others for guidance. I recently started working with a client who said: "I started on September 10, 2001 and it's been downhill ever since.' (P.S. Now he is moving in the right direction!)
h) Taking new action is often uncomfortable. Most people do not like feeling uncomfortable, so they don't do anything new. Please do not buy into this ignorance!
i) You choose to be confused, which is another way of not taking responsibility for figuring it out.

Behind all of our obstacles is FEAR. Ask yourself: what am I afraid of? What am I pretending?

Here are four final points to get you on the path of more referrals and the success you deserve:

1. **It all starts with self-awareness.**

   Change rarely happens without us realizing first what our current situation is. I truly hope this list helps next time you hear a great idea and do nothing (whether you were at a seminar, reading a book, or listening to an audio program). Don't you find it empowering to be reminded that change is often uncomfortable, that most people won't do it, and that if you do, you will start to grow as a person and move closer to your dreams and goals?

2. **Take full responsibility.**

   See the previous section!

3. **Align what you learn to what you value.**

   As motivated as I am to fulfill my potential in life, making lots of money for the sake of it does not inspire me. When I think back to the trade show area at the Wealth Expo where Tony Robbins spoke, I had no interest in the selling point "quick, easy money" that seemed to permeate the event and the vendors. Nobody suggested to me that my investment dollars would actually make a positive difference in people's lives. I was totally turned off.

   My point is: first you have to know what your obstacles are when you have a learning opportunity. Then you also have to align what you read with who you are and what you value otherwise you will not do anything. Congruency is everything.

4. **A new idea is not a bad idea.**

   Be aware that 80% of the time when we hear a new idea, we simply don't believe it. This does not mean it's a bad idea. Read on. Just like when you were 14 and you heard a new song, you did not buy it right away. As adults we need to hear something multiple times before we really like it and go out and "buy" it. The same may well be true for this book. This is a well-known advertising principle. You must see a television commercial at least five times before you remember it.

The more you are aware of your obstacles, the more likely you are to take action. Especially when you let the cost and impact of these obstacles sink in. Very few people are willing to slow down in life to take this time.

• • •

6. Get Comfortable Getting Uncomfortable

"80% of all people view growing pain as too uncomfortable or unacceptable. Only 20% recognize it as a learning experience."

— Denis Waitley

Asking for referrals makes many salespeople feel uncomfortable. While this book has as many suggestions and solutions as can be imagined to get past that, the reality may well still be that you have to face some fear if you are going to succeed! There is no quick fix alternative.

The only question is: how much do you want what you say you want? How motivated are you?

Take heart from some masters about the reality of being in the learning zone and outside the comfort zone:

"The quality of your life is in direct proportion to the amount of uncertainty you can comfortably live with."

— Tony Robbins

> *"The comfort zone is one of the greatest enemies of human potential."*
>
> — Brian Tracy

> *"Without uncertainty and the unknown, life is just the stale repetition of outworn memories...When you experience uncertainty, you are on the right path—so don't give it up."*
>
> — Deepak Chopra

> *"The more you seek security, the less of it you have. But the more you seek opportunity, the more likely it is that you will achieve the security you desire."*
>
> — Brian Tracy

Usually, getting out of our comfort zone means changing. Why don't we like to change?

In the excellent audio program, *The Aladdin Factor,* Mark Victor Hansen points out that *"We are creatures of habit. We get used to being a certain way, even if it doesn't work very well."*

This is an enormously important point. When we grow up, we get used to thinking and feeling a certain way in different situations. Regardless of whether this is positive or negative, it becomes our norm. Because it is our norm we get used to it, and it also becomes comfortable—even when it is negative or ho-hum. You might want to read that again.

Negative or mediocre mindsets can be comfortable for some people. I was astonished when I realized this was true for me one weekend when I was making no serious attempt to get out of an uninspired mood. I realized that in my dim and distant past, feeling that way was something I was used to. I was alarmed because I had fooled myself into thinking I was completely past that. I had also fooled myself into believing that it was comfortable and therefore a good thing! Only the dull pain of a nagging negativity clued me into the realization of how unmotivated I was feeling.

When it comes to pursuing more referrals, it is vital therefore to understand that just because we are used to our feelings and our comfort zone, the likelihood is that it is not helping us grow our business and meet all the people we need to meet.

In Susan Jeffers' *Feel the Fear and Do It Anyway,* she explains that fear will always be part of your life so long as you are growing personally and professionally—that this is a normal way to feel about new situations. Confronting them is the only solution, and this is better than living with the mediocre sensation that you're simply avoiding doing what matters most.

Doing something new can create anxiety and a crisis in confidence

The best suggestion I can make is that you step out of your comfort zone a few small steps at a time. Remember, growth only happens outside your comfort zone.

Even though change is a fact of life, many of us resist it and are frustrated every time it happens. Yet (as I'm sure you've heard many times!), if you keep doing what you've been doing, you'll keep getting what you've always gotten.

So first recognize what you are doing now that you a) want to stop doing, b) want to do less, c) want to continue doing, d) want to do more, and e) want to start doing. By the time you've finished this book, you should have several things to add to part e) and also be ready to spend less time on some other things that are comfortable but not getting you the referrals you want!

Second, once you recognize what you're doing now, ask yourself what's comfortable. Most of the time our habits and moods are a comfort zone for us and we do not realize it. Think back to how alive (and, yes, how scared) you felt when you first started in business. Nothing was comfortable, right? Then you let that muscle get flabby and untested. This all relates to self-awareness.

There are no secrets to success!

Third, moving past this discomfort (starting a new habit) takes a great deal of effort early on. Stephen Covey likens it to the needs of a rocket. Most of the energy it uses is required at take off and once it has done that, it needs very little to do all of the other remarkable things it needs to do. Similarly, as you launch some new habits that feel awkward, most of your effort will come at the start.

Ron was a client of mine for some time and we were spinning our wheels until I told him that if he wanted to succeed in his business, he was going to have to face his fear of prospecting and people saying no. Once he decided to face this almost every day, he started to make great strides, setting up more appointments, coffees – asking for what he wanted! He changed his mindset into seeing prospecting as a new challenge that could be fun – almost a game. It wasn't so easy that he felt this way all day long, but his new empowering mindset got him taking constructive action more and more consistently.

> *"The key to change is not more anxiety; it is more faith...in our vision and in ourselves...in others and in our relationships...in God and in everything else that gives us real strength."*
>
> — Robert Holden

• • •

7. Become Your #1 Fan

> *"The best way to get over feeling sorry for yourself is to appreciate yourself. If you sincerely love yourself and are truly proud of what you are, it becomes very difficult to feel like a victim."*
>
> — Dan Baker

Create empowering beliefs about asking based on the value you bring.

You need to truly believe in what you bring to the table. Why? So you know you deserve and therefore should expect referrals. There should be nothing more to think about unless the person you're asking is negatively disrupted by something else in his life or with the person you want him to talk to.

> *"If you believe in your value, how could it possibly be appropriate to hide it from people who need it?"*
>
> — T. Harv Eker

In his book, *Secrets of the Millionaire Mind,* Eker gives the following great example: If you had a cure for arthritis, would you hide it from others and let them either read your mind or guess that you had it? That's what most people do in their business by not having referral conversations.

Use that mindset to have more referral conversations; "*What would you think of someone who didn't offer suffering people their opportunity because they were too shy, too afraid, or too cool to promote?*"

Now granted, people suffering from arthritis are in more immediate pain than someone who needs a financial plan or an effective workout regimen, but given how disastrously many people manage their finances and their health, the concept is not a wild stretch if you think long-term. And if you think it is, change the word "suffering" in the quotation to "potentially needy" people.

Here are five beliefs you need to ask for referrals:

1. Your service is the among the best.

2. Your company is the one of the best.

3. You are one of the best.

4. Your clients are truly better off because of doing business with you.

5. Your clients benefit by recommending you because you are going to make them look good and get them positive feedback from those they refer!

DO IT! List all the value you bring to the table. Make this a long list of over 20 reasons that describe you and how you do business, perhaps things happy clients have said. Then add more to it! This essentially states: "I believe I'm really good at what I do and here's why." The more you reinforce this confidence the better, because you will find it easier to ask for referrals. You have to feel very good about what you do (and who you are) and that giving others the chance to recommend people they care about to you is the biggest no-brainer in the world.

Now, take some time to complete the list below. It is the first thing I expect new clients of mine to do. It may seem like too elementary of an exercise, but all communication starts with you. You have to be your #1 fan and confident in the difference you make. This is one way to get crystal clear about it. If you were going to list reasons why you should marry someone and could only come up with three, you'd be wise to reconsider! So think hard about this list. Often the most impactful ideas are the ones later in the list. Skip it at your peril!

20 Reasons Why People Should Do Business With Me:

1.
2.
3.
4.
5.
6.
7.
8.
9.
10.
11.
12.
13.
14.
15.
16.

17.
18.
19.
20.

Now, circle the 3 that resonate most loudly with you and keep these three top of mind somewhere – posted by your computer or on your bathroom mirror. Revisit this list regularly and keep adding to it. The goal here is for you to recognize all you do bring to the table so that you communicate in a compelling way. Remember: Sales is a transfer of enthusiasm!

Patrick, a client of mine, didn't have effective wording to get quality referrals when we first started working together, but he DID believe in his value. This gave him the confidence to ask for what he wanted. According to Albert Mehrabians' research at UCLA, only 7% of our communication is the words we use. 37% is the tone of voice, facial expressions and eye contact. 55% is our body language.

That means 93% of communication was working in Patrick's favor because after 8 years in the business, he realized he had a great deal to offer the people his clients knew. And his clients picked up on that belief because it was congruently communicated.

An insurance agent client of mine who had been in the business 25 years had never asked for referrals because he said he felt it was being pushy. So I decided to get under his skin a bit and asked: "Bob, why should anyone do business with you?" He looked a little ruffled, thought for a second, and said, "I'm better than 75% of the other agents out there!" Then a light bulb seemed to go on and he said, "That's the first time I've ever said out loud what value I bring to others." Now he's asking for referrals and behind his assistant's desk is a large sign he can see from his office that says "75" on it!

As soon as you have the conviction to look your clients in the eye and say; "I know I can help many of the people you care about," you're set (even if the words you use are softer).

<u>The Referral Mindset You Must Have:</u>

"I'm good at what I do. I can help people you care about. And I know I probably need to ask you."

That's it. Once you adopt this, asking for referrals continues to get easier until it's a completely obvious thing for you to do.

'I expect and deserve referrals from happy clients and people impressed by my help. I expect them because:

- (Insert your "I add value" here)
- I know my stuff, I am always getting better and learning more, I get very good feedback.
- I know that I will make them look good to whomever they refer me to because I will come through and do my absolute best for them, too.
- I am helping this person's family maintain their lifestyle, follow through on their dreams and stay in control/bring peace of mind
- I am offering them the chance to help other people's lives now and in the future.
- The information and experience I have is valuable to their future.
- (Followed by a belief that ensures you bounce back fast)
- If they don't want to refer me, they don't get it.

DO IT! Write out your 20 reasons and really buy into them. Put the Referral Mindset on a post it note or index card and put it somewhere highly visible.

Also I would highly recommend taking time at the end of each day to acknowledge yourself for all the things you did right. Some days I am so tired by the evening that I struggle to feel good until I do this exercise. It is really valuable!

CHAPTER 4:

Fearless Referral Asking

1. Identify Your Concerns with Asking for Referrals

> *"Asking—one of the most powerful success principles of all—is still a challenge that holds most people back."*
>
> — Jack Canfield, *The Success Principles*

Asking for what you want sounds so simple. Yet it is a real challenge for many because you have to confront your fear. Why are we afraid to ask?

I think there are many reasons. Often it is:

1. Fear of looking pushy
2. Fear of looking needy
3. Fear of looking foolish
4. **Mostly: fear of being rejected and hearing "no"**

When it comes to asking for referrals, other common concerns are:

1. Fear of sounding cheesy or canned
2. Fear of spoiling a good relationship
3. Uncertainty about when to ask
4. Uncertainty about what to say

Do any of these resonate for you? Being aware of why you are fearful or apprehensive is a mandatory place to start—provided you don't give it unnecessary validation. Stephen Covey warns: *"Argue for your weakness and it's yours."*

While these are the most frequently mentioned, there are plenty of other irrational things some people tell themselves.

Sometimes people need to talk for a few minutes about referral asking concerns before it 'pops' and they happen to mention something. Here are some things I've heard in the past:

> "Well for someone to refer me, they need to have seen the work that I do for at least a couple of years."
>
> "If I get paid by doing business with them, I feel like I've been compensated and shouldn't be asking for more."
>
> "I don't want my clients to feel like they're part-time salespeople for me."
>
> "I don't like making my clients feel uncomfortable" (even though it is YOU who are really the uncomfortable one making others feel the same way.)

Yet others have other concerns such as:

> "I don't want to lose the sale by asking them for something else."
>
> "I don't know how to retreat if the person is unwilling to suggest anyone."
>
> The most dangerous and unempowering: "If I just give great customer service, the referrals should come without me having to ask."

What are some ways to get over these fears so you can get more referrals?

a) **First, you've got to identify the unhelpful beliefs you have about asking. Make sure you have a clear understanding about why you don't ask.**

   Take 1-5 minutes and answer this: **What beliefs or concerns do I have about asking for referrals? Understanding this is crucial! Do not skip this question!** Be completely honest with yourself. You will make no progress without being clear what the enemy looks like!

b) **You must destroy the unhelpful belief.** Shoot it down by asking the following questions:

- What's silly about this belief?
- What is this belief costing me? (Really dig for pain!)

Why do you refer other professionals to people you care about?
That will reveal the qualities that really matter to you. When I do this with groups, the list is consistently short: honest, nice, competent, integrity/trust, punctual, good service, fair price, respectful, follows up promptly. Sometimes people add: likeable, experienced, sense of humor. Then look in the mirror. Do you fit that bill?
How do you match up? Look at that list like you're looking in the mirror. If you feel confident that you are all these things, that's great. Your next step is then to ask yourself: why then am I reluctant to ask? It doesn't make any sense, does it?!

What this really means is facing the truth: You are good enough. You do deserve to get referrals from others.

Also, if you don't refer much business to others, it's time to change. I find there is a direct correlation between the amount of business we refer and the amount we receive. I admit that adding value to others is what matters most, but referrals can play a key part in this. If you are untrusting by nature, I believe you subconsciously send the same message when *asking* for referrals. Re-read the Rule of Reciprocation!

Referral script #43, guaranteeing you feel like a used car salesman.

2. Keeping the Needy Spirits at Bay

> *"Neediness is a huge turn-off. In every situation in life, whether it's a business deal, a relationship or something you want, your power lies in letting go of any neediness. If you remind yourself that you don't need it—that you can survive without it and walk away if you have to—you will be powerful."*
>
> — Fiona Harrold

> *"More bad deals are signed and more sales are lost because of neediness than because of any other single factor."*
>
> — Jim Camp, *Start With No*

Coming across as needy is one of our biggest fears—and for a good reason: it kills opportunity. Overcoming it is so much easier said than done; believe me, I have felt needy for business more times than I would care to admit or remember. Knowing it comes with the territory does not make the pill any easier to swallow.

Neediness is selling just a little too hard (and where you're not coming from a place of sincere enthusiasm). It's putting product before relationship. It's pitching your wares before you even know much about the person you're talking to. It's shooting too soon before the other person knows, likes and trusts you enough.

There are so many body language cues that can give it away. It might be talking too fast, saying 'um' a lot, or failing to make enough eye contact. You might be wringing your hands unconsciously or swaying your body from side to side.

The tricky part is that we all develop relationships differently and don't know it! **We are not all created equally at establishing rapport with people.** Some people establish rapport quickly, while others take a bit longer. Most people have good intentions, but we all have very varied skill levels at having that recognized by others. You might want to read that last sentence again. It could be one reason why you are not getting the referral results you think you should be getting—others may not be recognizing the value that you think you're providing! That's one reason why some people have more success asking for referrals sooner than others.

We all know that we run and walk at different speeds. We can also accept that some people can carry a tune or draw better than us because we saw it from an early age. The only gymnastics move I could ever do was a forward roll (a "roley poley" was what we called them in England)—these skill levels are clear to all. But when it comes to building a relationship, that's harder to measure and notice. Our poor evaluation skills in this area lead us to believe that we are superior to others when the reality is very debatable.

Part of it is believing that you are making a difference; this gives you confidence. Part of it comes from knowing your stuff; that builds confidence. My coaching clients also share with me that it makes a big difference to have a referral strategy. And the final part of it comes from hearing from others that you have made a difference!

Sometimes you have to fake not being needy. I know I have. Every once in a while, that's just part of being self-employed or working on commission. Incoming business is not a consistent machine that churns out exactly the same opportunities. You have to be an optimist to succeed, and sometimes that means painting a rosier picture than is the reality that day. This is not my favorite point to make because I do not like to suggest you should be insincere, but the business reality is that nobody wants to buy tickets if they can see the rats running away from a ship that looks like it's sinking!

Also keep in mind that some people will never get it.

Remember the 20-60-20%? This may seem like an odd topic for the book that I should have some kind of disclaimer here, but not everyone you meet is going to recommend you. I've been in many a meeting with a client of mine who is frustrated about someone who is not forthcoming with referrals.

There are too many dynamics and intangibles at work in human relationships to be able to figure everything out or to insist that you have a 100% success rate.

As an optimist I do believe that some people who are initially wary can be warmed up and coached as they see the value and get to know, like, and trust you more. Nonetheless, don't resist too hard. You'll live longer being a tree that stays rooted but that gives a little when the wind blows!

• • •

3. How to Slay Your Fears of Asking

> *"Being rejected doesn't hold you back from anything. Only YOU hold yourself back."*
>
> —Jack Canfield

Rarely a day goes by in my life as a referral coach when someone doesn't express their fear of coming across as pushy. Ever have this concern? It's time to knock this on the head. Ready?

1. Get real. Slay the mythical beast called Pushy.

a) Walk through your last week and think of all the businesses you went into and people who called you: the bank, the dry cleaners, the coffee shop, the clothing store, the veterinarian, and the bookstore. What percentage of all the retail and salespeople you encountered were aggressive? Pause for a moment and really think hard.

How many tried to ram a product or service down your throat or up-sell you to death? You know, they were PUSHY.

Any? I can't remember the last time I had this experience – it's been quite a while. Sure, I get sales people calling on me, but nobody bugging me if I've told them no or not now. Almost all of them give up after leaving ONE message!

b) **Distinguish between assertive and aggressive**

I remember driving through central Iowa once (where let's just say the scenery is not very distracting) listening to a Brian Tracy audio and being startled by a distinction he made between the words:

PASSIVE – ASSERTIVE – AGGRESSIVE

Many people confuse assertive with aggressive yet they could not be more different. Both aggression and passivity are based in low self-confidence. Nobody walks away from an aggressive person feeling good. Aggressive is pushy, obnoxious, annoying, loud and rooted in low self-worth.

Many people say they are afraid to ask for referrals because they do not want to come across as pushy. I have never met anyone who had that fear who actually was a pushy individual. Have you? People who are really pushy are usually too blinkered to notice as they barge their way through life pressuring others to get what they want. And they are too insecure to admit it.

Conversely, being assertive is healthy. It's asking for what you want because you believe someone else will truly be better off because of your product or service.

It's asking for a free glass of water when you're thirsty. It's interrupting a conversation between two people in a coffee shop to see if you can plug in your computer by their table. That is not pushy. Avoid confusing the two.

I have never met anyone who told me they were afraid of being pushy who actually was! How about you?

c) **Think about someone you know that you consider pushy.** Is that how you run your business? Do you get feedback from people telling you that you're being pushy on a regular basis?

d) **Ask yourself: what's the worst that can happen if I ask for referrals?** Is that outcome really so bad? If you didn't have the business/date/job before you asked and you don't have it after, you've not lost anything.

So don't be afraid of rejection. It's a concept that holds no merit. You are not any worse off by asking and hearing no (since you didn't have it before you asked either).

As ice hockey great Wayne Gretzky said: *"You miss 100% of the shots you never take."*

So please, take a reality check. Like most of our fears, this one is almost always imagined.

e) Finally, people are not spending their day thinking about you, your call or your referral request. Remember, people think about themselves 95% of the time. Not you. Brian Tracy notes:

"Never do or refrain from doing something because you are concerned about what people might think about you. The fact is that nobody is even thinking about you at all."

If all else fails, remember the 18/40/60 rule!

When you're 18 years old, you are always worried about what others think of you.
When you're 40, you don't care what others think of you.
When you're 60, you realize nobody's been thinking about you the whole time!

2. Understand why you don't always ask for what you want so you realize that it has nothing to do with a fear of being "pushy."

In *The Aladdin Factor*, Jack Canfield and Mark Victor Hansen identify five possible reasons:

a) **Ignorance:** You don't know one or more of the following: what to ask for, who to ask, when to ask, or how to ask.

b) **Mistaken beliefs:** Example: I don't want to be seen as pushy or needy

c) **Fear is in control, especially fear of rejection and looking foolish.** Instead of taking action, *"we sit in judgment of others who are getting what they want."* Also, asking can make us feel vulnerable and that's not comfortable! (*See Chapter 3 from earlier: "Get Comfortable Getting Uncomfortable")*

d) **Pride:** we think we should be able to figure it out for ourselves. *"We are a nation of loners and self-sufficient do-it-yourselfers who will stoically suffer in silence to the end."*

e) **Low self-esteem:** according to Canfield, two-in-three adults suffer from low self-esteem.

3. Get under your own skin

Find ways to get some leverage on yourself. Ask someone else to hold you accountable for what you say you're going to do. It's one reason why high achievers hire a coach.

One of my favorite quotations comes from an interview that Peter Thomson has with Barry Hearn, who organizes major sporting events and manages professional athletes in the UK. Imagine an important meeting in your mind and say this to yourself:

"Why did you start doing what you're doing? Did you not begin with a dream? Did you not once want to be in the position that you're in now? All your life you've aimed towards a certain point. Are you going to blow it now by not believing in yourself when it's your whole life? How much do you want this?"

Here are some great questions to ask yourself:

- Why should I hide my value from people who could benefit from it?
- Why am I denying my prospects a great opportunity?

In other words, you are robbing the world of the contributions you can make!

...and if you can't believe any of this, you should find something else you can get passionate about. You can't fake it.

4. Believe in yourself, your company and your product/service.

YOU ARE WORTHY OF THEIR REFERRALS, OKAY? Part of people feeling awkward is when they don't believe in or use the product they're selling. **The more enthusiastic you are about what you do, the more success you will have.**

Learn from a 19 year-old. In Cameron Johnson's autobiography, *You Call the Shots*, he explains his philosophy that made him a multi-millionaire before he hit 20.
"My feeling is, I'd be doing my customers a disservice if I let them NOT buy my product. I'm always genuinely fascinated to know why people WOULDN'T want what I'm selling."

Many people will still not be interested, but that does not make you pushy. That's just the real world.

5. Like yourself more and more.

Liking yourself is another huge factor that makes the feeling of being pushy much less of a concern. Obviously this is a process for anyone. How important is it? Brian Tracy believes: *"The key determinant to success in sales and in life is how much you like yourself. The more you like yourself, the less you fear rejection."*

6. Be willing to fail.

The road to fulfilling your potential includes asking others for what you want. This also includes hearing people say no to you. (*See Chapter 3 from earlier, "Overcome the biggest myth in our culture."*) Simon Woodroffe, founder of YO! Sushi and one of the UK's best-known brands, counsels: *"It's not really until you're actually willing to walk into an office or pick up the phone and make the call where you might get rejected that you actually start to expand your business. The only thing successful entrepreneurs have in common is they are willing to fail."*

This is incredibly important. There is no short cut. Whatever you need to do to truly engrain this fact, do it!! Start by committing to one act of courage each day.

7. Develop a mindset that helps you bounce back from inevitable rejection and unreturned phone calls.

Have a snap response to put your mind back into the positive (or at least neutral). When it happens to me, I just hang up and say: "She doesn't get it!" or "He is totally missing the boat!" or "Their business must be going down the tubes." I remember asking Nate McCardell, a sales manager I know, what he said to himself as a successful producer when he was turned down. But I can't print what he said! The gist was that they had severe cognitive challenges!

I also like the expression SWSWSWSW: some will, some won't, so what, someone's waiting. It's a helpful phrase that describes the real world. There are plenty of opportunities out there if you follow the effective strategies of people who have truly had success, tweak them only a little as necessary, and persist.

80% of the people you interact with won't do business with you for one reason or another and if you can't handle that, you've made an interesting career choice! I believe that most people avoid that 80% like the plague and so are not asking much for business or referrals and blame it on not wanting to come across as the "typical pushy salesperson" that is mostly a figment of their imagination.

It doesn't really matter what you say to yourself so long as it helps you persist and deal with the challenging reality!

8. Know what you want and be specific when you ask!

This is Step 3 in the referral conversation (*see Chapter 6*). You can do everything right, but if you then say; "Well if you can think of someone else I should talk with, please have them give me a call!" you'll get few referrals.

9. **Take action in spite of your fears. Practice finding a way to ask that gets more comfortable with time—small steps outside your comfort zone.**

   Also ask yourself: what is the BEST that could happen? Focus your mind on what the BENEFITS are to the person asking. How does it benefit them? One study I read found that 85% of relationships were IMPROVED by making a referral. Maintain eye contact when you ask. Smile. Be respectful.

10. **Try humor. It can be VERY effective when it's authentic.**

    a) One client of mine, who had not been given a choice about attending my seminar, told me that he'd told a trusted client very sincerely: "Yeah my boss made me take this referral class, and now we're supposed to be asking everyone for referrals." After they'd had a good laugh at my expense, he got a great referral—an invitation to attend the annual convention of this person's trade association that October and get numerous personal introductions to prospects. Why was this person willing to do it? "Because I know you're not going to give anyone the hard sell."

    b) Another client of mine told one of her clients: "I know you've mentioned your two brothers before. I expect when you get together for baseball games, you spend most of the time talking about the beneficiaries on your life insurance policies (they laugh). Do you think they might be open to a quick conversation with me some time?"

    c) Sam Morton of 21st Century Media, a successful UK film maker I interviewed last year shared that he transitioned to asking by saying: "In my shameless business development mode: how about this idea and that idea?"

These ten strategies can help you make huge shifts in your business and your life towards asking with more courage and ultimately to seeing asking as a fun opportunity to help others! Only your actions will make a difference though so start today by asking for something specific that will move you forward towards your goals!

• • •

4. Make Asking a Habit and Pre-plan Your Asks.

I wanted to share something I have been doing that is a wonderfully effective habit and a best practice from one of my role models.

Every Saturday I do my weekly planning (*see Chapter* 7) and I have about 30 habits that I go through to make sure I am prepared and on top of things for the upcoming week.

One of the habits I have added more recently is something I've read about for years that's recommended by motivational speaker and author Jack Canfield. He swears by it and we all know we should do what successful people do if we want to get the same results as them.

As I look ahead to every meeting I have, I ask myself: "what do I want to ask this person for?" Options include: ask for their business, a referral, a speaking opportunity, that they consider subscribing to the *Loyalty Ezine* (my other business—see the back of the book for more on this or that they consider purchasing my new DVD or CD. The list can be endless. (For other ideas on what to ask for, also see Chapter 5: Start with Your Like List.)

Some months ago I met with Susan, someone I met years ago who's made more significant changes in her life than anyone I've ever known personally. For the exact same reason I am following Canfield's advice, I wondered what had helped her make such profound change. In other words my "ask" from her was broader: 'What have you done in recent years that has helped you become so successful?'

Susan recommended the Landmark Forum class offered by Landmark Education, which she said had helped her make some powerful breakthroughs in her life. I knew there were a couple of areas in my life where I was not getting the results I wanted on my own, and decided I should do the same. So I went back home, went online and signed up immediately. Little did I know how profound that would be! Yes, I would recommend their classes in a heartbeat. She also recommended a book by James Ray and I called a local bookstore and ordered that, too.

a. **Asking consistently must become a habit if you are to expect great results.**

Schedule the time to do it AND come up with an answer to "what could I ask him/her for?" It IS that simple.

b. **It's okay to start small.**

If you want to ease into this, start by asking for people's e-mail addresses or mailing addresses for your newsletter or for birthday cards. You could ask the person to attend your networking group as a guest, or for introductions to other centers of influence—and there's a soft way to do that. If you want to meet their CPA, you ask, "Can you recommend a good accountant?" People will tell you whether that person is good or not. They will not recommend them if they're not impressed.

If they say good things about the individual, "That would be a good person for me to know because if he and I work together, we can probably meet your needs better. Would you mind shooting him an e-mail and just suggest that you think it would be a good idea if he and I got together some time? Thanks."

While it's okay to start small, don't plan to stay there long if you'd like to stay in business! Do a better job with point 5 (below).

c. **Only ask if there's water in the well.**

You must make emotional bank account deposits in order to have earned the right to ask. Otherwise you will feel awkward and hurt the relationship.

d. **Don't ask the same person every time you see him/her.**

That would get annoying. You'll know too; it won't feel right.

e. **Asking more often means you must GIVE more often.**

Read this again! What's great about this habit is you have to think harder what YOU are bringing to the table. You can't ask if you haven't done anything for them lately! You have to keep adding value to the relationship by asking yourself the question: How can I most add value to this person?

You are forced to do a better job and keep raising the bar or else you have no right to ask. This is such a great win-win for the relationship and it keeps you on your toes. In addition, it keeps the relationship from getting TOO comfortable.

f. **Be specific when you ask.**

Don't ask for more money. Ask for $5,000. Don't ask for referrals to anyone they think might benefit, ask to meet Michelle Gonzalez, the VP at First National Bank. Don't ask your Higher Power to be a cool stud because you may end up on a wheel in Alaska! (*See Chapter 6 for more on this.*)

g. **Expect to get what you ask for.**

I admit this one takes some practice but I promise you it makes a big difference in what you say and the confidence with which you communicate.

A powerful way to practice this is to role-play. First you ask as if you are sure the person will say no. Get feedback on the words you used, your tone of voice and body language.

Then do it again knowing the person will say yes and get feedback on that too. It's a terrific way to get clear about how you're thinking and creating obstacles in your path.

h. **Persistence pays.**

Keep asking!

I would love to hear some stories from you about successes you get from simply making asking a habit. I cannot urge you more highly to truly turn this into a habit if it is not already. Most people wing it and that is not for you! May this bring you much joy!

DO IT! Put 10 minutes in your schedule to pre-plan your asks each week. Combine with Step 3 of the 6 Step Fearless Referral Conversation (see Chapter 6).

• • •

5. Fish for Referrals Before You Ask

How well do you 'fish' for referrals?

a. **Stop being so vague.**

One of the things that amazes me when I work with people on getting more referrals is how often I find people telling me that they don't know who they want that specific client to introduce them to. This is step 3 in my 6-step process. It's the most important step. I tend to hear vague responses like "oh, other business owners they know" or "some of their friends or neighbors—maybe some family members" or "I work better with women" (oh, you mean over 50% of the 300,000,000 people in this country?) (This is, by the way, one more reason to have a target market—this will be covered in my second book.)

The reason I'm so surprised is that we're talking about your next possible piece of business. It doesn't work to say "if you can think of someone else I should talk to, please have them give me a call." It doesn't work to say "who else do you know that I should be talking to?" You've got to be more specific.

Your job is to narrow down your referral request to 2 or 3 people. Your clients are crazy busy just like everyone else. The odds of them spending time figuring out who among the 200 plus people they know that they should introduce you to are very slim.

It is YOUR RESPONSIBILITY to identify specific people you'd like to be referred to. Only a few raving fans will do it for you.

b. **You belong to one of two types of people when it comes to hearing referral opportunities:**

One group will have one ear listening out in case other business opportunities are mentioned.

The other group is 100% focused on the task at hand and any such opportunities go in one ear and out the other.

This is not a criticism but **if you fall into the second group and you do not know other people your clients know, it's time to get more curious! You are missing out on the chance to help a lot of people and do more business.**

Learn from Walt Disney: "Curiosity keeps leading us down new paths."

c. **Your job is to FISH using "FORD" and to make this a HABIT.**

You've got to take a few minutes here and there to inquire about other people in their lives. FORD is an acronym I heard about from the Ninja Selling program for Realtors.

F: Family and friends: Who do they spend free time with? Who are they close to?
O: Occupation: Who do they work closely with at their company? Who are their best clients? What synergistic professionals do they work closely with? Who are the primary suppliers to their industry? Where do they get their new business?
R: Recreation and hobbies: What activities and organizations are they involved in?
D: Dreams and goals: What do they hope to accomplish in the next 12 months? What plans are they making for the future?

If your memory is like most people's, write this information down. It will always be helpful for conversation in the future and tells your client that you cared enough to remember.

d. **Leverage the "liking" and "comfort" factors.**

Liking: Listen for how much your client likes a certain person when they talk about him or her. If you can hear in their voice that they're not too fond of their boss, how do you think it's going to be for your client to want to refer you to that person?

If your client tells you that you should talk to someone in their HR department, you might want to find out who they like the most in HR even if it that person may not be the decision maker. Your advocate will get you a warmer referral and, because you're leveraging strong relationships, your end result will be much more favorable.

It is common sense: If someone likes you, they're more likely to help you out.

Comfort: It's critical to ask yourself not only who do I want them to introduce me to, but also: **To whom would this client be more comfortable referring me?**

We have to think about the types of conversations real people actually have and how we can incorporate what we do into that. It's our responsibility. If our referral source doesn't know what to say to introduce us, he or she is not going to say anything! Now, there's nothing wrong with asking for your client's guidance on this.

If you are a financial advisor, would your client be more comfortable discussing ways you can help co-workers in a professional business setting, or their family? Some families don't talk about money or insurance with each other. Others know it is a vital topic to discuss. Your job is deciding which direction to take that referral conversation by playing detective a little and getting a sense of what your client would be more willing to do.

These two factors matter so much because the more they work in your favor, the easier it is for your referral source to recommend you.

If you want more referrals, you must be fishing as often as humanly possible. It's your next piece of business and, if you're doing a good job and your client likes you, you've got someone right there who can help you!

• • •

6. It's How You Ask for Referrals

> *"Customers don't care about you. The only thing customers care about are themselves and their problem. Rainmakers say 'you'; they don't say 'I'."*
>
> — Jeffrey Fox, *How to Become a Rainmaker*

A referral request should be *client-centered* not one that focuses on you growing your business.

Word your referral request as often as possible in a way for clients to be focusing on how they can help people they care about. **It's almost NEVER about you! The wording must focus on your client and people that matter to them.**

Avoid lines like:

"I get paid in two ways."

"I grow my business by referrals and was wondering who else you think I should talk to."

"I am trying to increase my business and would like your help."

Avoid the "me, me, me" approach! It turns people off and sounds needy.

(These lines only work on occasion with sympathetic family members and very close friends, and even then how well they endorse you is questionable because they may doubt your competence. Also, if you have been in business for a long time and have excellent relationships, you can ask for help and get results—it's counter-intuitive and works. You have enough emotional bank account deposits to pull this off.)

In his book *How to Become a Rainmaker,* Jeffrey Fox makes the point that most of the time people don't care about what we do. At best it is polite conversation. Otherwise, people are not generally thinking about us.

It is more effective to appeal to what matters in the life of your client than to hope he or she is deeply concerned with seeing your business succeed.

Really, when you left your last dental appointment, did you spend any time the rest of the day fretting about whether they were still going to be in business the next time you went back for a cleaning? What are the last few restaurants you visited? Has the thought ever crossed your mind that they might not be there in a month, so you took action to help?

Think about most of the businesses you patronize. If they don't ask you for referrals (and I'm sure most of them don't), how much time do you spend thinking of other people you should recommend them to? It's almost a ridiculous question, yet that's exactly what this book is designed to address and why there's such a need for it! Almost no one is doing it well!

DO IT! Think about how you are currently asking. Is it all about you, or all about them? The solution: find wording that works: The 6 Steps to a Fearless Referral Conversation.

• • •

7. Don't Shoot Too Soon.

> *"Like any good fighter pilot, top salespeople know when to shoot."*
>
> —Thomas J Stanley, *Networking with Millionaires*

Before explaining when is the best time to ask, a few words on when not to ask.

1. **When you're not close to having earned the referral, do not ask too soon.**

   This isn't a science. Sometimes people's discomfort with asking comes from knowing the relationship isn't strong or they really haven't brought much value.

   I was sitting with a financial advisor this week who was telling me he rarely asked during an early appointment with a client. Wanting to hear *him* tell me, I asked him why not. He said; "I haven't brought much value. I wouldn't recommend me at that point!"

   Especially in the financial and insurance services, many new reps shoot too soon. They are often trained to ask right away because getting referrals is so important. Unfortunately most of their client relationships are not strong enough from a business credibility standpoint to earn referrals, so it creates awkwardness on both sides, rejection, and—sooner rather than later—the rep gives up because it feels wrong. They are tired of getting a bloody nose. Ironically, many reps probably give up right around the time they should start asking!

   New sales reps need to be trained on exceeding expectations, consistently adding more value and be asking themselves; "what can I do to be more liked and trusted by this person?"

2. **You will usually need to wait until you have some business credibility.**

   You can ask friends or family for help but they too will usually need to know you're quickly becoming competent. People are understandably wary about putting their integrity on the line when integrity is the foundation upon which our character and values are based. That's the power of a word-of-mouth endorsement.

Unfortunately when you are starting out, client relationships are seldom strong enough from a business credibility standpoint to earn referrals.

If you are a new salesperson, you are likely meeting with people who may know you well and trust you on a personal level, but often they do not have a lot of confidence in you professionally. Your prospect may still have you labeled as the kid down the street who used to mow their lawn, or as what you did in a previous career. I know when I first started my business, my family had me pegged still as a teacher somehow "playing" at something else for a while. It took about four years and a postcard from a speaking engagement 1,000 miles from my home before they started taking me seriously!

So what do you do if you are new? Diffuse these concerns by explaining how much you are learning, how much expertise you have at your fingertips and of goals that lay out the grand future you see before you. Talk as though success for you is simply a matter of time. Confidence is a magnet.

3. **Do not ask at every meeting you have.**

It is always smart to have referrals on your mind.
It is always smart to plant seeds about referrals.
It is **not** smart to ask for referrals every time you see people. You will get annoying. And people will not go to bat for you unless they are clear that you have done a great job. Any names you get will be mostly worthless and those people will not return your calls.

DO IT! Whenever you're in doubt, ask yourself: If I had to give this relationship a "grade," what would it be? What do I need to do to get this relationship to a B+ or an A? How else can I add value to this person? (Often this will not relate to your business) Then you'll be ready to ask and get what you ask for.

• • •

8. The Right Time to Ask and the Best Time to Ask For Referrals?

> *"My simple formula for knowing when to ask for referrals is 'when value has been given and value has been recognized'."*
>
> — Bill Cates

It's all about value: Remember, referrals must be earned! The right time to ask is simply when your client is happiest.

1. **It can be during a formal meeting with a client.**
   Use the 6 Steps to a Fearless Referral Conversation (*see Chapter 6*).

2. **It could be on the phone as you inquire about some value you added to him or her. Give first. Then receive.**

   The other person's guard is down because you have another reason to call that adds value to him or her. You are building the relationship further.

   I would urge you to rack your brain and think of as many creative ways as possible to call people and make emotional bank account deposits. It could easily be to follow up on value you added in another way—a referral you sent them or some sales ideas that you e-mailed.

   This isn't just some technique. The relationship has to be there. Read that again! The relationship has to be there! You can't forward one e-newsletter to that person and call expecting instant referrals. People will see right through any ruse. But if you truly care about that person and make deposits, those referral requests get easier.

   Here's an example of what you might say on a call. In Keith Ferrazzi's most recent book, *Who's Got Your Back*, he describes the order of such a conversation very simply as "Give. Get. Repeat":

   Step One: Give
   "Crystal, I'm calling for two reasons. First, I was curious how things worked out with (my referral to you) Nicole?"

Crystal responds.

"Good! I'm glad that worked out. I thought you two would connect and find some areas to be able to help each other."

Step Two: Get

"The other reason I'm calling is I wanted to ask you: how well do you know Sondra Hicks? Would you be willing to put in a good word for me with her because I have been helping a lot of executives in similar situations? Really all you need to tell her is that I specialize in working with executive teams, that you'd recommend that she at least have a quick conversation with me, and find out if I can give her a call some time."

3. **It could be during a lunch, coffee or beer meeting where you have provided value.**
   All the same rules apply as above.

4. **Listen to your gut.**
   Sometimes you just know you've established good rapport and can ask for what you want. This sense usually develops with experience.

5. **Ask after you've added value and your client has acknowledged it.**

Step 2 of the 6 Step Referral Conversation (*Chapter 6*) helps you determine if you've brought value and earned the referral. If it's obvious at other times, great! The only reason I'd suggest waiting until later in the meeting is if it seems too off topic during a meeting that is meant to focus on your client.

Note: You can add value early and often and, on occasion, early in the relationship can sometimes be the best time to ask! Why? Because you have given your client something that's truly worth talking about!

A past client of mine in California, Jenna, is one exception to the rule about not asking too soon. She does such a great job at creating a wow first impression that she gets most of her referrals early on in her client relationships. This happens because her financial planning process is truly holistic and is one her clients have never experienced before—so they talk about it to others. Also she is a master at managing the experience by offering fresh-baked chocolate chip cookies and serving gourmet coffee in china cups.

Here's another example. Recently I switched chiropractors—I'm on my fifth. I've seen four over the past 16 years with fair to disappointing results. My new chiropractor, Corinne, takes a holistic approach (I was a little skeptical about what exactly that meant) and does far more than simply adjust my back. She spends most of the time working on my ligaments and muscles that support the adjustments. She also discusses nutrition, specific exercises, and how the events in our life manifest themselves in our bodies as physical symptoms. One of the first things she told me was that her goal was not to have to see me more than a few times—the exact opposite of what I've heard from every other chiropractor.

I felt so dramatically different and better after just that first appointment that I raved about her to three people that same day. What's scary is that just a week later I was already used to feeling that much better and it was no longer a daily talking point. In other words, sometimes the best time to leverage referrals is early and often—but only after you have earned it with such an impressive first experience.

6. The best time to ask is after the meeting is over

Dave was a client of mine who wanted to work with more veterinarians. He had one such client up to that point, and was having lunch with the office manager of that clinic. His first request was that she call other clinics in the area to recommend the workshop he had done on disability insurance, but she looked uncomfortable about doing that. So he dropped the topic and they talked about other things.

As he was sitting in his car with the door open about to say goodbye, he transitioned back to his referral request: "Gail, what *would* be the best way to find out how I might be able to help some of the other vets around here?" She thought for a moment and said:

"Aren't you having a booth at our convention in a couple of months?"

He said he was and so she came up with the idea: "Well, why don't I introduce you to some people then?" The quality of his referral opportunity went from asking for a warmed up call (50%) to a personal introduction (80%)! The story got better. Two months later, it turned out that Gail was presenting at the convention and as she wrapped up, she told her audience: "And if you ever want a great workshop for your clinic on disability insurance, talk to Dave Edmundson over there. He did a terrific job for us!" Close to 30 people gave him their contact information.

I like this time to ask because the other person is more relaxed. The meeting is over, you know you've done a good job, and you've transitioned the conversation. Now you're talking about what that person is doing over the weekend or on some other safe personal topic that's not upsetting to him or her.

THEN you pivot back to business:

Step One:

"Oh by the way, when we were talking earlier, you'd mentioned (and now you get specific):

a) Speaking at a company event
b) That your parents live nearby
c) That you thought your business partner might benefit from doing the kind of work we've been doing.
d) That your cousin was moving to the area

Step Two:

a) How would you recommend setting up something like that?
b) What would be the best way to find out if they'd be open to a quick conversation with me some time?
c) Do you think the three of us should have lunch sometime?"
d) Do you think she might be open to me connecting with her about her real estate needs/search?

DO IT! I know this last step is a technique. However, it works for a reason and it works when your request is sincere.

CHAPTER 5:

Fearless Referral-Getting Strategies

1. Where Does Your Referral Business Come From?

Two years ago, I was having coffee in Worcester, England with a man named Richard, then a director of the G.M.G., an organization that hired me to do a couple of referral seminars for its members – all small business owners in synergistic industries. While talking to him about his own company over the previous few weeks, I had asked him three questions. He told me that his answers had helped him enormously in determining where he wanted to focus for that upcoming year. Perhaps they'll help you, too.

Question 1: Where exactly has all of your business come from over the past 12 months?

Richard knew he was getting most of his business from referrals, but he was startled to see that in the past three years ALL his business had come from referrals.

Identifying specifically who has recommended you is a helpful reality check. Some professionals and clients you know may well be ones you like a great deal and even enjoy spending business time with, but they are not actually helping your business grow. You need to be aware of who these people are.

Conversely, there are quiet-spoken individuals who are out there endorsing you and you are barely noticing.

Question 2: Who are your top referral sources?

What also surprised Richard was that it was only 10% of his clients who had referred him business in the past three years (along with some other centers of influence). He had never asked any of them for referrals even though he'd been in business for more than 25 years. As I dug to find out if he'd done anything to find referrals, he did say that he told stories to clients to "drop hints" about other companies he wanted to do business with.

For example, if he was talking with a happy client who knew the owner of the BMW dealership, he would mention how he was working with the owner of the Audi dealership in the hope that his client would connect the dots. I am sure there are occasions when this helped. However, the numbers don't lie: 10%!

The real points here are:

a) How many of your clients are you asking?
b) If you're not, why not?
c) What are you going to do differently over the next three months to improve the relationships you have so you can ask confidently and comfortably?
d) What are you doing to keep your top referral relationships strong and flourishing?

Question 3: WHY are they your top referral sources?

This was also a revelation to Richard. "I noticed from looking at the names that my top referral sources were almost all projects with overseas companies, and that I had spent lots of time with these people. Lots of quality time on planes, at their offices and over meals. It was the personal connection we made on these projects. The 10% are the ones I got along best with. We became friends." Remember the Likeability Factor? Richard was getting referred by the companies that had gotten to know him better and realized what a great guy he was.

What a huge discovery!

Step Two for Richard was to then ask himself: How can I spend more time with my clients and do less work virtually so they can get to know me better as a person? **How can I find more ways to be face to face with my clients to build those relationships?**

Can you relate to that one?

Question 3 is so important, and it's essential that you do this exercise. Who gives you the most business and why? What difference did you make with that referral source that they like you as much as they do to refer you? The truth is you gave first before you received and you likely gave a great deal. Here's how I developed one of my first great referral sources:

Tim was a new insurance agent when I met him in a leads group. His wife was pregnant with their first child, and he was working hard in his business and not getting his desired results. He was working 12-14 hour days and was questioning what he was doing wrong. His confidence was at an all-time low. So that's what we addressed first. I told him to identify the time in his life when he was most confident, what he was doing in all areas of his life, and what else made that time so memorable. We also talked about physiology and how we carry ourselves during times of struggles compared to times of great confidence.

The time Tim hit upon (and by the way it rarely takes long for people to know when this time was) was a specific year in college when he had his own radio show and had asked out Ann, the woman he married. Music had been really important to him at that point in his life. He realized that he had been shutting that out as if it wasn't somehow appropriate now that he was a business owner.

Changes he made immediately included leaving his office and sitting in his car to play a fun tune whenever something happened that really frustrated him. He put pictures on his desk of the ultrasounds of Ann and their daughter. He started keeping a journal of what he was grateful for; I still remember him telling me about a Vietnam veteran that was in his office who had such a rough life since the war and how his own struggles paled by comparison. He quickly became aware of his body language and posture. He started walking with more confidence, keeping his chin elevated and his shoulders back. He focused on his body language in client meetings by sitting forward and listening intently. Clients could sense the confidence, and therefore he began to sell more…to the tune of doubling his agency's production.

We also came up with new business strategies and his numbers continued to grow. Within nine months, he not only became a father, but also a Top 100 agent, a prestigious award for new agents in the largest car insurance company in the country. Within three years he was managing new agents elsewhere in the country showing them how to run an effective business. Since then he has already been promoted twice more.

Some of my best referral sources are people I met at pivotal stages in their business, either early on or where their frustration level was to the point where they knew they had to make some positive changes. I am sure you will find the same—that you met certain clients at a crucial time in their lives and therefore they really appreciate how you helped them. For others, it may be specific ways you excelled in customer service and/or how you treated them – all things you can replicate with all your clients once you're aware of their power and what they are! A client of mine got referrals this past holiday season from top clients by personally taking gift baskets to them. Obviously he'll do something next year to impress them as much.

DO IT! Go though these three questions so you can make sure you focus on your referral sources better.

• • •

2. Start with your "Like List."

One of the best ways to jump start getting more referrals is to do what I recommend to all the people I coach when we start working together: put together a Like List.

Why is this so important? Remember Robert Cialdini's Rule of Liking says that when people like you, they want to say yes to you (*Chapter 1*).

So leverage the best people (arguably the low hanging fruit) and make it easy for them. **This means you must be crystal clear about what you are asking for—so clear that the person you're asking doesn't have to think about who you want to meet.**

1. Take 20 minutes and write a list of all the people who like you the most. It will likely be very similar to a list of people you like the most!

2. Write down what you would like to ask that person for.

Your first tendency may well be to think about doing business with that person. That's a perfectly good option (see point 4 below). I would also urge you to think bigger and more creatively than this.

a) Perhaps your contact works for a company whose employees could use your help.
b) Maybe he or she is on a team or in a department that would be a better request.
c) Perhaps you could ask to interview that person because he or she belongs to a target market that would be a great niche for your business.
d) Could you ask for an introduction to one of their centers of influence (COI) since that person could open up new doors for you?
e) What about a possible speaking opportunity to do a workshop?
f) Or maybe this person networks in a powerhouse organization that you would love to be invited to as his or her guest.

Don't just think about immediate business. Many of these ideas could bring you far more revenue in the long term.

Remember: people are more defensive when they think you are targeting them. Often you are more likely to get business with that person by telling stories about the work you have done and how you have helped others like them. It is innate for people to personalize what they are hearing, so as you describe clients who are happy because you helped them with something, your audience is going to be thinking about themselves. (They will think about themselves provided that they see themselves as being in a similar situation. It wouldn't work to tell a new business owner how you help affluent physicians. They will think you're talking about a different species).

Last year, a client of mine called a couple of his friends from his Like List who were veterinarians. His "ask" was for their advice on how to target market that profession. He spent quite a bit of time explaining to them how he helped vets with their finances and protecting their businesses. By the end of the conversation, both of them blurted out: "Gosh David, it sounds like I really should meet with you too!"

g) Use the "Ask the Expert" option (*see Chapter 6 for more detail*).

When you are talking to your contact, ask: "What would be the best way to find out if this is something that might be really valuable to the other partners in your firm/industry?"

If you're not currently using this question, you're missing out. It works extremely well with people who like you so long as you ask in a sincere, curious way.

h) Make it an ultimate goal to have that contact be a client. The reason it is usually better if that person is a client is they know your work even better, and that makes it easier for them to endorse you. A referral is usually more compelling when you can say you are a client too. It's similar to the concept of you selling a product you use yourself versus trying to sell a product you don't use. The credibility is higher.

   My insurance agent finds it very easy to send business to his Realtor COI when he tells his customers: "If you don't have a Realtor that you trust, you should talk to Trent (shows them Trent's card). He helped me and my wife find a home a couple of years ago. My wife, Erica, is pretty cynical and asks a lot of tough questions and she thought he was great—so you don't even need to take my word for it! Would you be interested in hearing from him?"

3. Once you have the names and the information you requested, then the only decision is to decide how you want to ask to maximize the chances you'll get a yes (a phone call or in person—not e-mail!). Face to face is usually better not least because it's harder for people to say no!

DO IT! Putting together a Like List is one of the actions I would recommend more than almost any other in the book as somewhere to start.

• • •

3. E-mail? Pick Up the Bloody Phone!

> *"Although the internet has often been referred to as the information superhighway, might the lack of personal contact between negotiating parties be more like a roadblock than a route to successful outcomes?"*
>
> —Goldstein, Martin & Cialdini

In this age of virtual communication and challenges with reaching people by phone, it's tempting to resort to e-mail for most communication—including referral requests. I know that different generations seem to have different preferences about communication. How does e-mail help and hinder our referral business?

1. E-mailing people is usually a way to avoid being rejected.

After all, do you know anyone who does not own a phone? People find it much harder to tell you "no" when you are face to face with them. They also find it harder to say no when you are on the phone because at least then you are a real person.

With e-mail, it seems we are treating people more and more like we do other motorists on the road. They are not people with personalities that we hold open a door for; they are maniacs in speedy machines putting our lives at risk. They cease to be ordinary people with everyday challenges. It's the same as people who e-mail us. They become rabid salespeople interrupting our days, evenings, and weekends.

Referral requests by e-mail should be a last resort unless you have been instructed that this is the best way to reach someone. Despite my aversion to e-mail, of course I use it too. It works well when you are very confident that you will receive a reply. But you must honestly ask yourself: How often is that?

The rule is: Pick up the bloody phone! (It's a permanent appendage to your body anyway, and besides, you probably sleep with it by your pillow!)

2. "Can you e-mail me something about that?" is almost now the modern day equivalent of being pushed aside with a "can you send me some information? (which I will then throw away unopened as soon as it arrives!)"

From a referral standpoint, avoid email, push for a personal meeting or at least a phone conference call.

What does the (surprisingly extensive) research say about e-mail?

3. E-mail is less effective for persuading others.

Why? **Miscommunication is more likely**. The 15 studies cited in *YES!* by Goldstein, Martin and Cialdini find six quite significant challenges with using e-mail compared with a face to face or telephone conversation.

a) All the non-verbal cues (voice inflection and physical gestures) are missing. Remember: more than half of our communication is non-verbal (eye-contact, gestures) and that another 38% is the tone of our voice. Only 7% of our impact is determined by the words we use. OUCH for e-mail!
b) The meaning of your message is harder to interpret—especially sarcasm, seriousness, anger, and sadness.
c) Senders of e-mail are usually unaware that a message can be misunderstood. We rarely take the time to re-read our e-mails carefully before we send them. Even when we do, we rarely ask ourselves; "Could the person I'm sending this to interpret this content in a way I don't mean?" This issue is never going to get any easier given the growing volume of our inboxes.
d) People are less likely to exchange personal information in an e-mail that helps to build rapport. No relationship, no referrals.
e) Women are even less persuaded by e-mail than men.
f) We are increasingly likely to be interacting with people from cultures and countries different from our own where being curt in our communication will hinder us further.

4. Mass e-mailing for a favor rarely works.

Mass e-mails create a diffusion of responsibility so that nobody steps up to the plate. It is too impersonal. Individuals do not feel like they are being addressed.

5. It's easier for people to put off your e-mail request.

Why? **Because one of the six universal principles of influence is commitment/consistency** (*see Chapter 6*). This means we want to act consistently with our commitments and values. When people tell you to your face that they will follow through on a referral they've mentioned, they feel a much greater sense of obligation to do so.

6. Sometimes an e-mail can work fine.

Bryan, a client I'm currently working with, does have success getting his referral sources to warm up their referrals by e-mail (*Step 5 in the 6 steps covered in the next chapter*). His assistant, Ryan, forwards them a pre-written paragraph of what to say with permission for them to change it however they see fit.

DO IT! If you are asking for a referral, do it in person whenever humanly possible or by phone.

• • •

4. Use an Agenda

What's the #1 excuse people use for not asking for referrals?
"I always forget to ask."

Most of the time, what they *really mean* is:
"I am not comfortable asking."

Getting comfortable asking is the most important piece to developing a thriving referral business. That's what chapters 1-4 address.

Using a written agenda for meetings provides one solution to those who are comfortable asking for referrals or who are at least getting more comfortable. Although, come to think if it, even if you are not asking for referrals, your business will benefit. I promise.

Having a formal agenda may sound pretty trivial; but for many of you reading this, it is not (I'm not going to waste your time or mine here!).

There are many reasons to have a written agenda. Few top sales professionals are naturally organized and few have the time to want to spend on creating agendas. But I believe it is another tool that will help you get more referrals.

*A sample skeleton agenda and script are below.

The Advantages to Using an Agenda:

1. From a referral standpoint, the intent here is to plant the seed that there is more to the meeting than just what may be obvious (see sample below) and that there will be some kind of 'value discussion' that you can use to pivot to having a referral conversation provided your client is happy,

2. Using an agenda will help to make sure you commit to including a value discussion and not forget again or run the meeting too long.

3. It will help you see a referral conversation as a way you can bring more value to your client by giving them a chance to look good by recommending someone as good as you (and not seeing it as a time to focus on your needs—this is a very important and empowering paradigm). Being given referrals should build relationships.

4. It sets a different tone. Try using an agenda at least for a period of time. I have never heard someone say they regretted using one. It will not *transform* your meetings, but many people say it sets a more professional tone. It may seem a bit stuffy to a few of you, but most people like dealing with organized professionals. No client fully respects and prefers paying someone who flies by the seat of

his pants on a regular basis—even though you seem to think it is fun. It respects their time more and allows for a discussion on other priorities that may have changed since your last correspondence.

Your clients like to know what to expect and will appreciate it, even if it's only subconscious. They will feel more comfortable. Remember: certainty is a fundamental human need.

5. It will help you confront your real fears behind asking for referrals and help you start asking more effectively.

A few tips about agendas:

1. **Make them simple and very easy to duplicate OR delegate them to someone else.** If you're saying to yourself: "Matt, this doesn't fit with my personality," re-read the advantages, see if you really have these covered already and keep reading.

2. **Give your client a copy of it,** preferably one that's **exactly the same** so it looks like you are both literally on the same page and that you're not hiding anything.

   Note: If you are still perfecting your referral conversation and need written reminders for yourself (and you think you need to put them on your version of the agenda), try to keep them as brief and simple as possible and remove them as soon as you remember.

3. **Consider e-mailing or mailing your agenda out ahead of time.** This looks very professional and organized and, most importantly, gives your client a chance to make sure you are both on the same page and doesn't surprise you when he or she walks in the door with a topic you're not prepared for.

4. **With prospects, have a conversation at the start of your meeting about how that person heard about you.** Regardless of what they say, it gives you a chance to say something like, "That's unusual! Pretty much everyone I work with these days was referred to me by someone else."

Or "most of my business comes from people saying nice things about me to other people." You are planting some seeds here. If most of your business comes from personal recommendations, that makes a statement to them about how well you run your business and that many others have felt strongly enough to put their integrity on the line to refer others to you.

5. **Focus on the client.** The wording and items in general on your agenda should focus on the client, not you.

6. **Don't use the "R" word.** Put Value Discussion/Conversation/Check-in on your agenda. Do NOT use the word referrals on your agenda. This word is DEAD; it does not resonate positively with the general public anymore. It's like the word "used"; used cars became pre-owned cars and more recently are being called pre-driven cars. Next they will be called pre-touched or pre-sat down in... You get the point.

   Since you cannot have a referral conversation and ask for referrals unless you have earned them, first you need to verify that you have. The best way to do this is to have a conversation about what the biggest benefit/s have been to your client (*see Step 2 in Chapter 6*).

   Therefore, call (what you want to become) your referral conversation something like "Value Discussion" (my favorite), "feedback" or perhaps "customer service update." Some sales people I know have put on their agendas "Clients Helping Friends Program," "Helping Others" or "Other Ways We Help People You Care About." All of these can be effective *provided you are comfortable with them.*

   I am not an advocate for calling it anything more obvious (such as "Introductions," "Personal Recommendations" or anything tacky that more or less says "Help Me Grow My Business"). This is partly because today's consumer is more aware of older school sales techniques and because they scream the "me, me, me" approach. It turns people off.

7. You'll notice that the value discussion does not come last on the agenda. You don't want to run out of time. Again, the healthiest mindset is that the discussion is not intended to benefit you (it will, but your client doesn't care about that) but to make your client look good by recommending you. In other words, recommending you is a value-added service. For example, it's like the time you recommended a friend to your chiropractor and she returned delighted because of how much better her back felt. How did you feel after that?

8. Item 7 on the sample agenda that follows is intended as the assumed close—that you expect them to do business with you. You can still reduce the prospect's resistance by telling them; *"If you think this looks like a good fit for you, then we'll schedule our next appointment. If you don't think this is best for you, we won't; but hopefully you'll at least have learned something beneficial. How does that sound?"*

   But you still have *your* expectation firmly in black and white on the agenda.

9. Lastly, a client of mine, Rich, taught me that if you don't like the word 'agenda,' call it 'discussion outline.'

SAMPLE AGENDA FOR INITIAL MEETING

Name: ______________________________ Date: ______________
How did you hear about me?

1. Tell me about you. Update your info. Your expectations.
2. (optional) Why me/ABC Company or About me
3. Your objectives for today's meeting:
   a)
   b)
   c)
4. Other ways I can help you: (list)
5. Value conversation
6. Q&A
7. Schedule next appointment/annual review

Sample Agenda Script

"Before we get started, I'd just like to go over the agenda quickly. Oh, and do you still have 'till 3pm? Great. Well first off, I want to make sure we have all your contact information up to date and I would like to know a little bit about you and find out what your expectations are of me. Then the primary reason for our meeting today is to take a look at your (ex.) investment goals and see if there are any better ways that suit your needs than what you are already doing. After that I'd like to quickly go over a few other ways I can help you, have a brief (what I call) 'value discussion' to make sure this was a good use of your time, answer any remaining questions you have, and then, if everything looks good to us, schedule your next appointment. How does that sound?"

DO IT! Make up a simple generic agenda that you can start using, print off 50 copies of it and see how it helps to set a calmer, more professional tone to your meetings.

• • •

5. Have an Expectations Discussion

> *"We create many negative situations by simply assuming that our expectations are self-evident, and that they are clearly understood and shared by other people."*
>
> —Stephen Covey

Do you know everything your clients expect from you? Do *they* know everything *you* expect from them? Consider having an expectations discussion to express your value, minimize miscommunication, and increase referrals. Here's how.

Several years ago was I having lunch with a CPA friend of mine who was casually explaining to me that he told all his prospective clients that he expected them to send him business if they were going to work together. *Really?* I had heard this from many top producers before. Finally the light bulb went on in my head. Why can't we all do this?

Perhaps we can. The road to getting there is to have a two part "expectations discussion" in which, provided that you meet their expectations, clients will refer new prospects to you. If you already have a lot of existing clients, integrating this into your conversations is no problem: It's never too late to revisit how you are doing. But you can also take this approach upfront with new prospects and the feedback you get can even help your with client retention.

1. Why expectations matter

Don't you feel better when you know what to expect? Generally speaking, people like certainty. When you fly somewhere the pilot tells you how long the flight is, which route you'll be taking, what altitude you'll be flying at, what the movie is, etc. If only my dentist would do the same. Whenever I go, he doesn't explain what he's going to do or how long anything is going to take. When the drilling starts, all I can do is white-knuckle my hands, think about lying on a beach somewhere, try to recall how many fillings I'm scheduled to have, and pray the agony will be over soon; it is *awful*. Don't put your clients through this!

2. Beginning the conversation

Here's my solution: *Really impress them with everything you bring to the table.* Set yourself apart by being exceptionally professional and making them feel very comfortable. We all like to know what to expect. Below is part one of a sample conversation that allows you to find out your client's expectations of you. Keep in mind this is a sample version that you would want to personalize:

YOU: Before we really get into our meeting today, I'd like to find out a little bit more about what your expectations are from us potentially working together. What are you looking for in a good financial advisor?

(I think it is better to pause here and let them respond because they will not be able to think of much.)

YOU: Thanks. That's all good to know. I've put together a list of some things that other clients have said they expect from me. I'm curious: what else on this list is something you also consider to be important?

Have Prospect look over the list and identify other things that matter to him/her:

1. Have integrity and to work in YOUR best interest.
2. To care about you, your assets, and your financial security.
3. To look out for you and bring a sense of control to your financial situation and help create more confidence about the future.
4. To ask questions and listen well to truly understand your needs and goals.
5. Consistently provide high-quality service regardless of how much you invest.
6. Bring more balance to your financial life and help you do the things you need to do for your future (whether you feel like it or not!).
7. Provide my financial expertise and experience, and stay current on changes in the investment world that you don't have the time to do.
8. Put in the time that you probably don't have to devote to your accounts/portfolio/policies.
9. Buy you lunch once every year.
10. Be your financial coach.
11. Give you 100% of my best effort.
12. Help you reduce your taxes, if possible.
13. Help you with other insurance and investment needs.
14. Meet with you at least quarterly/annually for financial reviews.
15. Probably not be in a very good mood if (insert your favorite team) lost last weekend!
16. Return your phone calls as soon as possible (always within 24 hours).
17. Utilize all of my resources (including my assistant/team) to best handle your concerns, questions, and requests.
18. Advocate for your business.
19. Make sure your investments fit with your own principles, values, and risk tolerance.
20. Serve as your financial advisor for the long term.

"Can you think of anything else that's really important to you?"
"How does this sound?"

The key ingredients—and why they work

Clearly you need to personalize the list to fit your business, your niche, and even your sense of humor. One financial advisor included "provide unbiased advice even though I'm a Dallas Cowboys fan." A Realtor I know put "fresh farm eggs every once in a while." I think it's important to have a little humor in it so you don't come across as too heavy and for the prospect to think, "She's got a good sense of humor; she seems pretty nice." Here's why this approach works:

You can counter objections. One other thing that makes this a clever approach is that you can include a counter to every objection you've ever heard from someone who didn't work with you in your list. In other words, close people on whatever concerns they might have but might not verbalize. A prospect thinks you look rather young? Tell them your clients expect fresh, innovative ideas backed by a company with reputable expertise. Tell them your clients expect enthusiasm and stellar client service that is above and beyond what they could normally expect from a veteran in your industry. Tell them you specialize in serving the needs of clients in their industry and have more experience than many veterans in working with people in their profession. Find what clients may perceive is your weakness, and make it your strength.

You set yourself apart. More than anything, you will really set yourself apart by having this conversation! If you don't believe me, you should try being on the receiving end of an expectations discussion.

It's important to allow prospects time to think of their own concerns and to give them time to talk about the list and what they like about it.

My personal favorite is #18. Can you imagine going to a bank to open an account and hearing, *"Sarah, I'm fortunate enough to know a lot of people in this community. Another thing you can expect from me—once I know a little bit more about you and your business—is that I would be happy to introduce you to some people who might want to do business with you."* You're hearing about ways to make money for your business and saying to yourself, "I thought I was here to get sold something!"

You set up an "emotional bank account" Based on author Stephen Covey's "Emotional Bank Account" concept, this conversation lays out expectations and begins the relationship on solid ground. The premise of the emotional bank account is that without you clearly explaining what value you bring from the start, personality clashes and communication breakdowns can result. People judge us based on their expectations of us, and most of the time these are only implicit and have not been discussed.

Part two of the conversation: Your expectations

Now that you've clarified what the prospect expects from you and you've impressed them with all that you bring to the table, now it's your turn to lay out your expectations. Once again, you will want to tweak the wording to fit your personality, what you do, and words you would use:

YOU: Great! Well now I'm clear on what matters to you, there are a FEW things that I ask for in return.

I ask..... (READ the list out loud)

1. That you laugh at my jokes.
2. That you arrive within 10 minutes of all scheduled meetings or call.
3. That you return my calls within 24-48 hours.
4. That you come prepared with all necessary documentation.
5. That provided that I meet all of your expectations, that you think about people important to you in your life (whether that's at work or in your family) and recommend that they at least have a conversation with me to make sure (for example) they have all their ducks in a row.
6. That you let me know of any significant changes in your life, or goal changes.
7. That you mostly follow my recommendations.
8. That you at least fake an interest in fishing if I start talking about it.

Does that sound fair enough?"

What I love about this part of the discussion is that you're no longer a needy salesperson. You're confidently asserting that you have expectations for a healthy working relationship. I'd suggest that your list be much shorter than what the prospect can expect from you, and that you start out with a couple of very light requests. This portion of the conversation allows you to:

Plant the seeds for future referrals whenever value is provided. The real intent of this part of the conversation is #5. Once you've stated it, it gives you permission to return to it any time whether it's the next day, week, month, or year. *"Michelle, do you remember the discussion we had the first time we met? How am I doing? (Am I doing what I said I would do for you?)"*

Once you've verified that you are indeed doing a great job, *"I don't know if you remember this, but one of the things I asked from you was that if I was meeting your expectations, that in return you would think of people you care about and suggest that they have a quick conversation with me to (for example) make sure they have all their ducks in a row."*

Determine that you are living up to their expectations. By the way, if for some reason you don't hear great things, move to plan B. Rather than ask for referrals, simply ask how you need to improve and address it immediately. That's how raving fans are won.

Once you have consent for referrals, use Steps 3-6 in the 6 Step Conversation in Chapter 6.

Get confirmation that your expectations are reasonable. Once you've covered #5 from your expectations list, continue on without a pause to the final two points. Remember to finish by getting their consent that your expectations are reasonable.

DO IT! Have an expectations discussion that fits your business and your niche. It will go a long way toward building trust, and position you as an upfront professional who isn't afraid to have tough discussions. These discussions prevent misunderstandings and give you a way to communicate your experience and the value you provide clients.

CHAPTER 6:

The 6 Steps to a Fearless Referral Conversation

1. Follow the 6 Steps to a Fearless Referral Conversation

These six steps are ones I have tested over the years and that my clients find to be the most effective way to get high-quality referrals on a consistent basis.

The good news is that they are easy to understand. However, it does take some practice to implement them and get results. You should also note that skipping more than one or two of them can lead to no referrals at all. Remember, if getting referrals were that easy, everyone would already do it and you wouldn't be reading this book!

I am reminded of a time I was traveling in the Netherlands and I learned enough Dutch to walk into a McDonalds and order a sundae (I guess small things impressed me when I was 20!). So I knew enough to get what I wanted. The only problem was I didn't understand anything else I was asked! Did I want nuts on the sundae? Was my order for here or to go? Nor would I have understood the amount I owed except by then the woman behind the counter was speaking English to me! The six-step referral conversation is the same way. Using a bit of it will help but will not get you all you need.

My advice is this: implement steps one and two right away. As you feel comfortable and competent with them, add another step at a time.

Here are the six steps in brief.

Step 1: Acknowledge Your Client.

This is your opportunity to powerfully commend your client. Recognition and acknowledgment is the No. #1 human need we have after food, clothing, and shelter. It sets the right tone for a potential referral request.

Step 2: Have a Value Conversation.

"What has been most valuable about the work we've done so far?" Have you helped your client reach a personal goal? Put them on the path to financial security? Having a value conversation helps you determine if you have earned the referral. You only ask if you have.

Step 3: Get Specific and Ask the Expert.

It is your job to help the client identify one to three specific people who might be open to a quick conversation. This is the most important step, and it's not one that comes easily. Most people who ask lose the opportunity for a referral by saying: "If you know anyone else I should talk to, please have them give me call." You need to be much more specific.

Step 4: Reassure Your Client.

Reassuring your client gets worked into the conversation in the wording of Step 3. Your clients often need to hear from you that they are not expected to know the needs of their friends/associates. It helps reduce their resistance and apprehension.

Step 5: Coach Your Client on What to Say.

It is your job to make sure the referral source has something simple and effective to say to the person they are referring. Most people do not know how to introduce you, and this way the referral opportunity is not lost because they either say the wrong thing or (more likely) get cold feet and say nothing.

Step 6: Keep Control of the Process.

You cannot simply hope your contact information will be passed on so you can sit by the phone and wait for it to ring. You need to make sure you have control of the next step. You need to follow up with your client first to see if the referral has been "warmed up" and wants to talk to you. Getting this permission increases the client's responsibility to following through and avoids issues with "Do Not Call."

• • •

2. Use Step 1: Acknowledge your Client

"Never underestimate the long-term influence of filling others' buckets... Every time you fill a bucket, you're setting something in motion."

—Tom Rath & Donald Clifton

"I never yet met a person who didn't want to be appreciated."

— Mary Kay Ash

Based on all the research and every study ever done of what it takes to be successful and fulfilled in our society, exceptional people—like you and those in our network—are either in the top 10% of their industry or moving that way. How do I know this? Because only people such as yourselves—the elite top ten percent—take the time to read sales literature like this and develop themselves professionally and personally. This isn't just some clichéd sales advice: read almost any autobiography of a top performer from Serena Williams to Jeffrey Gitomer to Stephen King. They are students of their field *and* they take action on what they learn. You already have one of the most challenging jobs in our society dealing with rejection and setbacks daily, so through your persistence, learning and action, you put yourself in the top 10% if not this year then in the next 3-7 years.

There. That's me acknowledging you and I mean every word of it.

The purpose of Step One is to commend your clients for the smart decisions they have made.

People love it. Even if they have made some poor choices in the past, they will appreciate you highlighting what they got right.

Taking time to acknowledge others is POWERFUL. I learned this idea from a sales manager named Dutch. If there is a secret weapon to improving relationships quickly, this is it. Robert Cialdini might call it complimenting people, but rather than saying "my, what brown eyes you've got," the goal is to be factual about identifying a trait or action that has produced positive results.

In 1896 it was Henry Ford talking to Thomas Edison (who was his next door neighbor). He was explaining how he was developing a gasoline car. Edison thumped the table and exclaimed not only that it was a great idea but also explained why he felt that way. Ford was later to write: "That bang on the table was worth worlds to me. No man up to then had given me any encouragement.., here, all at once, and out of a clear sky, the greatest inventive genius in the world had given me complete approval."

Today things are no different. People are crying out for positive recognition. This is why recent best-selling authors, such as Tim Sanders and Keith Ferrazzi, are such strong advocates for open, authentic and meaningful relationships in the workplace. Proof of this is demonstrated in Tom Rath and Donald Clifton's *How Full is Your Bucket?* They cite Gallup research, which found two things: a) lack of recognition is the No. #1 reason why Americans leave their jobs; and b) 65% of Americans received no recognition in the workplace in 2003! Lack of income actually came in fifth place. Once you start getting good at this, you will be surprised by how much others appreciate your feedback.

This is not some fake exercise about glossing over something unsightly. People will see through that. But for you to put some thought into what your client has done that many other people haven't will be received with sincere gratitude. After all, since 50,000 thoughts go through our heads each day, and on average 80% of them are negative, we can be assured that most people spend much of their time berating themselves.

There are three rules to your acknowledgment:

1. **It must be sincere**
2. **It must be specific**
3. **It must be true**

This is not as easy as it may sound. There's a reason why few people do this already and do it well. For those of you who are naturally empathic, you probably already do this. But you are in a small minority. For most of us, it takes practice—quite a lot of practice. I have found this a difficult skill to master.

If ten of us were to put this book down right now and go and coach soccer to a group of 12 year-olds, the "feedback" about eight of us would give them at the end would likely be something general such as "good job guys—well played." It's the business equivalent of "thanks for coming in today; it was nice to see you." This is empty, white bread content that provides no useful feedback.

But to take the time to think of specific actions and character traits demonstrated is altogether different—and the other person knows it too. What specific things has this person done that merit recognition above what every other person does in a similar situation? **In other words: what does this person do that most would consider above and beyond?**

- What qualities did this person need to make the specific wise choices that they did?
- In other words can you acknowledge them for their courage or persistence?
- Where did they show self-discipline or sacrifice instead of making an easier choice?
- Where did they take a higher level of responsibility compared to others?

Everyone goes to greater lengths and takes creditable actions with one of their passions—is it with their children? Their pet? A hobby? A service project? Can this relate to your line of work or conversations you might have with that person? Even my hairdresser, Brittany, pointed out to me that not many people would spend five hours on a Saturday to work on their book. That made me feel acknowledged.

Matt Loverine, one of my recent clients, is so effective at Step 1 that he will often be given referrals on the spot. He makes people feel so good about themselves for the wise decisions they have made, that their brain instantly starts to think of others who would like to feel the same way. "You should talk to the other guys in my department," a client will say or "You know, my sister should meet with you." I cannot tell you this happens often for other people, but I do believe that much of that is because most people are really weak at the skill of acknowledging others!

I remember Matt sharing with me one example in which he was working with a client who had just been downsized from a car plant after 30 years. This man had saved his money over the years, and Matt shared with him his utter disbelief that some of this auto worker's peers had done the same yet decided to spend their savings rather than re-invest it. As he slapped his own knee to emphasize how crazy he thought this was, he said: "I met with two of your co-workers. One of them blew all his money on a Harley after he was let go, and the other decided to spend 22 years of his carefully set-aside savings and blow it all on a trip to Vegas!! Believe me: you will be so happy with yourself five years from now—and as you hit 70 and 80 years old."

Ideally strive to make the other person feel as though he or she is in a small minority of the population who makes smart decisions.

If you have third-party statistics, I would recommend using them because then you won't sound biased or like you are making something up.

Example 1: "Before we wrap up, I want to take a moment to commend you for deciding to take proactive steps about your retirement future today. I'm sure there were more fun things you could have done with this time, but that's why successful people are willing to do the things unsuccessful people are not, even though successful people don't feel like doing those things either!

Amazingly, 55% of Americans with retirement plans are receiving no professional guidance. They are walking around blind. Kudos to you for taking the bull by the horns and getting yourself out of a potentially perilous situation. Ignorance is not always bliss."

The next example makes general reference to the three areas the client has made decisions on—which can be an effective strategy:

Example 2: "Before we talk about next steps here, I want to acknowledge you for taking the action you have. Procrastinating on the decisions we have made about your estate, your legacy, and how you want to invest in the next five years would have been easy to do. It's easy to ignore something like long-term planning when you're as busy as I know you are, but this is precisely the kind of planning that too many people ignore and then regret later in life.

I came across a fairly recent article the other day (in a 2004 Journal of Political Economy) which reported that the average American (58%) spends more time picking out a new tennis racket or TV set than deciding on their contribution rate and investment allocation on a retirement plan. So I hope you realize how wise this time investment has been!"

DO IT! Everybody likes recognition. You've likely heard the expression "feedback is the breakfast of champions". I first read it in Spencer Johnson's The One Minute Manager. This is your opportunity to say positive things to your client for making some good decisions.

And, very importantly, now you are talking to someone who is feeling very good about himself, it is your turn to ask for positive feedback.

• • •

3. Use Step 2: Have a Value Conversation

> *"The more you get your prospects and clients to articulate the value they see, the more clear they become about the value."*
>
> — Bill Cates

The purpose of Step 2 is to find out what value your clients have received. You will hear in the tone of their voices how pleased they are and whether you have earned the referral (or not).

The focus here is to get **positive** feedback that builds on the feel-good factor of Step 1. People refer you when they are most happy with the work you have done. I first read about this idea from the referral training veteran, Bill Cates. The point of this question is to hear whether you have a green light to ask about referrals. **Remember, the 6 Steps are a train of thought**—not something contrived. You only ask for referrals if the client is happy.

You are not asking for feedback, in general. Get that some other time! If the person is not that thrilled with what you have done, you will hear qualification in their voice when you ask—so you don't need to worry that this is an artificial exercise. If there is something you sense they are concerned about, go ahead and find out what it is because asking for referrals at that point would be a mistake!

The Value Conversation question is:
"I'm always curious to find out: What has been most valuable about the work that we have done so far?"

Two things:

a) **Be silent and let them talk!**
b) **DIG!** Feel free to ask, **"Anything else besides that?"** after the client responds. The more value they can verbalize, the better. One reason this is important is because many people need time to think hard to give you the highest quality answer. The first words that come out of their mouths might not be the most meaningful.

The most important thing in this conversation:

- You want to get them **talking about how they FEEL**.
- Don't be afraid to ask in addition: How do you feel about what we've done?
- The ultimate feeling is peace of mind—even if they don't use those exact words. We are more giving when we feel good and we want them to give more referrals!
- It feels good to get this feedback and it makes the asking easier!! Even if you know the client is already happy, the feedback you get can still be valuable and may teach you what your clients consider most useful compared with your own opinion.

Some other ideas about the value conversation:

- **Feel free to re-word the question slightly** if you prefer the words "helpful, useful, important" etc. You could even ask:

  "What has been the #1 takeaway for you from our meeting today/the work we've done together over the past four years?"

Or "what have you gotten most out of our meetings so far?"

- **The question must be open-ended:** Don't say "Was the meeting helpful? Good. Now, who else should I speak with?" One reason for this is most people are polite and will simply nod their heads to avoid looking rude or to avoid a potential confrontation. It will not give you an accurate response.

- **Avoid: How am I doing?** People do not know how to respond to a question such as this. They say "fine." Nobody is going to go to bat for you and recommend you to others based on just feeling "fine"!

- **Write down what your clients say for feedback.** Using their words when making your referral request will be much more impactful than saying something generic like; "Who else might benefit from talking to me?"

- **Take notes.** If your client seems a little unsure what to say, it pays to take notes during your meetings and make a mental note of instances where you believe you brought value, education, and ideas because many of us will forget—especially if the relationship has been going on for a while. In fact, most people have a terrible memory for where they were when they started with you and we do have this tendency to fool ourselves into thinking that we made most of the progress on our own. Remind them in a super-nice way of the actual reality!

- **Provided you get a really positive response, you have earned the right to have a referral conversation. If it's less than very positive, you should not attempt to ask for referrals.** You can't quick fix relationships. Don't waste your time or theirs and push the relationship in the wrong direction. Instead, find out how you can better serve this person, address it, and most likely they will then become raving fans because you actually cared enough to listen and respond. There's a reason every success story ever written includes the message: "Press on: Nothing in the world can take the place of persistence."

Example 1:

You: "I'm always curious to find out: What has been most valuable for you about the work that we've done together?"

Client: I like the fact you're easy to work with; you're relaxed. Well, and I trust your advice. You know your stuff.

You: Thank you! Anything else besides that?

Client: You always get back to us quickly. I like that. And I feel like I can call you any time—that's nice, especially since I don't think much about finances except on the weekends.

(Now the value conversation is over, the green light is on, and it's time to transition to Step 3. Remember, you don't have to ask in the very next sentence. You could end the meeting right now and wait until you are packing up or on your way out—so long as you have enough time.)

You: I appreciate that; I know it's important. Last time we met you mentioned Gabe, your brother-in-law in Colorado, and that he wasn't too happy with his current advisor. How would you recommend finding out if he might be open to connecting with me at some point?

Example 2:

Consultant: "I'm always curious to find out: What has been most valuable for you about the work that we've done together?"

Client: It's been very helpful. I'm glad to have a plan in place for my family and know they'll be taken care of—whatever happens.

Consultant: I'm glad to hear that. Anything else besides that?

Client: Well, I think you do a good job of explaining everything. I've had experiences in the past where the person I was meeting with would—well, I'd just get confused—and I felt awkward admitting I didn't really understand what they were saying.

Consultant: Yes, I try not to bamboozle folks!

Client: And I'd also have to say that you asked me some really important questions that I had not considered, so I think what we came up with is very strong.

Consultant: How do you feel about that?!

Client: A lot better!!

(Now the value conversation is over, the green light is on, and it's time to transition to Step 3. Remember, you don't have to ask in the very next sentence. You could end the meeting right now and wait until you are packing up or on your way out—so long as you have enough time.)

Consultant: I'm happy to hear that. You know, I'd really like to meet your business partner, Al. I don't know if you guys talk about this kind of planning much, but he sounds like a neat guy, and I can at the very least make sure he has a plan in place for his family like you do. What would be the best way to find out if he might be interested in connecting with me some time?

Do you always need to have a value conversation? I don't think so. There are times when your intuition is strong enough that you just plain know that your client is really pleased with your work. Often there may be dead giveaway things they say, and sometimes there may be more subtle exclamations such as, "Really?" (I didn't know that) or "That's really helpful." If in any doubt, you've nothing to lose by having a value conversation.

DO IT! At your very next meeting. This is the easiest step to start doing right away!

• • •

4. Step 3: Why You Must Get Specific

> *"When we ask people if they "know anyone who..." we are giving them much too large a frame of reference, a blurry collage of 250 faces will run through their mind, but no individual will be singled out. They may feel frustrated, as though they let you down."*
>
> — Bob Burg, *Endless Referrals*

The purpose of Step 3 is for YOU to identify who you would like your client to introduce you to (it's not their job).

Most of the time by "specific," I mean that you are asking about 1-3 actual people who easily come to your client's mind.

STEP 3 IS THE MOST IMPORTANT STEP OF ALL. You can do everything right and get no referrals because you are being too vague about whom you would like to help.

First you need to understand why you are afraid to get specific. The so-called logic is that lots of people would benefit from meeting you (I don't doubt that this is true!) and that if you keep it nice and general, you cast a wide net and increase your chances of there being a few fish at the end of the day.

Unfortunately the shot gun approach backfires on the human brain, which needs focus and simplicity to identify a target for you. It's one reason why there are no referrals for people who tell others they can help "any small to medium-sized business" or that "if you know anyone looking to buy or sell in the next six months, have them give me a call." Nothing sticks in the mind. There is nothing for the brain to focus on.

Second, there are two reasons you need to get so specific that the person you are talking to narrows down options in his or her brain to two or three people.

> **Reason #1: The average person knows too many people** (200-250, whether they realize it or not) and they need your help

to think of someone specific. Well, who comes to your mind when I ask you these questions?

- Do you know anyone who might benefit from my services?
- Do you know anyone who likes sports?
- Do you know anyone who likes to grill out in the summertime?
- Do you know any business owners I could help?
- Do you know anyone that would like to reduce their stress by getting more referrals?
- Do you know anyone who would like to make more money by getting more referrals?

So, are you tripping over names left and right and scrambling to write them down and send them to me?

Or were you overwhelmed by a fog because so many people fit that bill that you've no idea where to start?

Your clients are exactly the same. **You've got to make it EASY for them!!**

> **Reason #2: Everybody is CRAZY BUSY** and they are not going to talk to eight different people for you. They don't have time. If they don't leave the meeting with someone in mind, very few of them are going to spend any more time trying to think of "anyone." If you like to think you're different and that your clients do think about you frequently, consider these questions:

I can't emphasize this enough: **STEP 3 IS THE MOST IMPORTANT STEP OF ALL.**

Never again say: "If you can think of anyone who can benefit from my services, please have them give me a call"

When you use the word "anyone," they will think of no one!

"Do you know anyone else I should be talking to in a similar situation to yours?" It's almost always too vague. Get specific!

It didn't work in 1493, either.

5. Use Step 3: Ask Directly For a Specific Person

Once again, the purpose of Step 3 is for YOU to identify specifically who you would like your client to introduce you to (IT IS NOT THEIR JOB!).

So what are the best ways to get specific? There are two effective ways to transition immediately from Step 2, the value conversation. One is to ask directly about a specific person and the other is to ask the expert, your client.

As soon as the other person is done giving you great feedback and it is clear good value has been recognized by them, you say: "Thanks for that (feedback)" and you move straight into your next train of thought—helping someone else:

Directly ask for the person you want to meet. Make sure it is someone they like!

Example 1: "In the past you've mentioned that you know Megan Gibbs pretty well. Now, I don't know if the two of you ever talk about the type of work we've done together (Step 4), but:

> *"I would really appreciate you introducing us."*

Alternative versions could be:

> *"I'd love to meet her. Is there any chance you could set up a lunch for the three of us some time?"* or

> *"I think I could really help her in similar ways that we've worked together. Do you think she might be open to talking with me about (for example) her financial goals/this kind of planning process?"*

Now, hopefully you've been doing your fishing and pre-planning your asks because this will make Step 3 so much easier and it will make you feel much more confident. Here are five other ways to help you get more specific:

a) **Listen out for and write down specific individuals they mention:**

Re-read the section in Chapter 4 on fishing for referrals. Write down names that come up because clearly you want to find the right time to bring them up again.

Doing this sounds so simple and obvious, but what I've found is that **it is not obvious to everyone**. Many salespeople are so focused on what they are explaining that **they are not listening** for what some could mistakenly consider to be irrelevant asides.

I used to think everyone listened out, but one day I was making this observation to an insurance agent and he gave me a completely blank look. In his mind, if he was explaining homeowner's policy coverage options to a customer, he was doing it 100%. He did not have 10% of his radar out should they mention other people = potential business opportunities.

Now when I mention this to audiences, EVERYONE gives me a blank look because those who do it think everyone does it and those who don't do it have no idea what I'm talking about!!

b) **Educate your clients on what a qualified referral is. Seek out a clear SIMILARITY that will narrow down the choice to 1-3 people!**

The transition statement from Step 2 is "Thanks! It's interesting: what I've found recently is that **the people I can help the most are..."**

- *Or "I've been working lately with a lot of people like you who are..."*
- *Or "I've really been specializing lately on working with other people who are..."*

Same life situation as you: just had a baby, just got downsized, very close to retirement, seeking a new job, just got married, families with special needs children, recently widowed

Same profession: ex. architects, dairy farmers, also business owners of companies with more than x# employees (likely in the same industry)

Same job title: HR directors (even better: in the paper industry)

Same demographic: Indian physicians, also residents of Sunny Pines neighborhood

Same religion: Lutheran men 50-65, on your banners committee at church

Same employer: employees at Xerox

Same pastime: also curious about income properties

Same frustration/pain: with the turnover at their current bank, with the service they're getting from their current cell phone provider, always having to go back for more chiropractic adjustments

Same life challenge: know they don't have the time or expertise to work on this.

c) **Pre-prepare a list of prospects to present to your potential referral source.**

Overall this approach works well if you are comfortable using it. I feel it is more natural to have sourced names through conversation, but I know that's not always possible for everyone, and I know using a list works because I've had plenty of clients who have success with it!

The internet can be a great source of information for finding connections. A company website might have a list of industries it serves or testimonials from happy clients—sometimes even a client list. Being connected on "LinkedIn" or other social networking sites can also be a way of seeing whom someone is connected to—although just because they are on someone's page, it doesn't mean the relationship is strong. Be sensitive to that when you bring it up.

Eric Heiting runs a financial planning practice named Physician Wealth Strategies. His clients are almost all doctors and are so busy that they are rarely going to make the time to call referrals and recommend him. He has great success showing them a list of references of doctors who have given him permission to use their name and then shows the new client a list of other physicians in their department. Then he asks a specific question: "Is there anyone here from your department who started quite recently?" Or he might ask: "Who else from your department has a stay-at-home spouse?" Or "Who else from your department has children in high school?"

Pat Marget is Managing Director of Executive Benefits Network, a company that specializes in working with banks. He has had success presenting a list of other banks that are in the same state to his current client and asking that bank president: "I'd really like to be able to help others in the same way. From this list, where else do you have good connections where you might be comfortable putting in a good word for me?"

Peggy David is the marketing director for her husband Jerry's business. He works mostly with business owners. Whenever he has an upcoming meeting with one of them where he knows he has brought good value (Step 2), she researches the internet for similar businesses to the one owned by the person Jerry is about to meet. Then he has three separate questions: "I do have another quick question for you:

- "How well do you know any of these people?"
- "Could you tell me a little bit about them?"
- "Now, I don't expect you to know how happy they are with their current advisor (step 4), but would you be willing to introduce me to any of them?"

Then he uses Steps 5 and 6.

Chris Anderson used to specialize in helping teachers with their retirement planning and had similar success with that approach. Everyone has favorite co-workers, and there are always new staff members to help.

Be sensitive to the flip side. I have trained in companies where some of the salespeople were uncomfortable about being asked to talk to a client and producing a list of their neighbors! I don't blame them. And that shouldn't be necessary. A conversation can usually elicit who is important in that person's life.

The list is also helpful when there are a lot of people to choose from or to jog someone's memory:

"These are a number of local companies I've identified as ones I can really help. Do you have any contacts at any of these?" I recommend this highly if you're in a networking group that meets regularly.

d) **Use "generic" specifics such as sibling, favorite co-worker, best friend rather than family, friends, business associates (too vague).**

These help to narrow it down and work much better. The overly vague 'friends, family members and co-workers' is too much. Nobody is going to talk to 15 co-workers but they might talk to 1 or 2. I urge you to try this.

e) **Have a "new car" conversation**

While this is more of a technique and not one I hear about much anymore, depending on your business you might find this idea useful.

"You know how when you buy a new car, you suddenly notice how everyone else seems to be driving the same car as you. It's rather like when... (give an example such as being pregnant, being on crutches etc). Well now that you're starting a family/investing in income property, you probably seem to be talking to other people who are in the same situation..."

There is no reason you should ever hear, "I can't think of anyone" ever again!

If you are hearing this, go back and re-read the section on fishing for referrals and the whole above segment. Your client isn't going to come up with names. If you want referrals, it's your job to do your homework.

The Importance of Being Specific

6. Use Step 3: Or, Ask the Expert!

> *"People will support that which they help create. When you dictate even the most thoughtful and logical concept to a person—this idea is still a command. When you ask her to contribute to its inception, that very same idea becomes a 'personal crusade.' "*
>
> — Mary Kay Ash

> *"Really think about it: How do you feel when someone you care about asks for your opinion? Do you get annoyed? Do you feel put upon? No way—it's an honor! People love to feel that their counsel is valued, that they're making a difference to each other, that they're needed and appreciated."*
>
> — Keith Ferrazzi

I love this approach and it works really well!

Remember: Step 3 is about working with your client to identify who you can help next. That's it: Who's next?

Example 1: Dr. Lee works at ABC Clinic where one of his benefits is $400,000 in life insurance. His wife is a stay-at-home mother. According to Thomas J. Stanley's research in *Marketing to the Affluent*, 9 in 10 physicians do a very poor job managing their finances. Most doctors need closer to $2 million to $3 million to be properly covered. If Dr. Lee were to die prematurely, his wife would be in a really challenging situation.

My point here is that when you "Ask the Expert," you are safely assuming that there are many other people in the same situation in that client's affinity group that likely could use the help (usually a work department, team members, other partners in the firm, other nurses on the ward, other teachers in the same grade level, other board members, etc.)

YOU: "Thanks for the feedback (transition from Step 2). One of the things I'm curious about, Dr. Lee, is I can't imagine that you are the only physician in your department who only had the $400,000 of insurance coverage. Now I'm guessing *you don't spend much time discussing different types of life insurance with your colleagues (Step 4), but:*

> ***What would be the best way to find out if this is something that might be of value to the other physicians in your department?"***

Then you close your mouth and wait expectantly for a helpful response.

Example 2: Your software company has just had great feedback from a title company client.

> *"That's great to hear. I'm delighted you're so pleased. You know, it would be fun to work with some other title companies on this kind of thing. I don't expect you would know the needs of other companies necessarily (Step 4), but:*

How would you recommend finding out who else might be interested in our software program?"

Here's why "Asking the Expert" works so well:

a) **Everyone likes to be treated as an expert. And it makes them feel good and you not feel needy about asking!**

   People like it when you ask them for advice. This is different than asking for help from a place of weakness. You are generating their suggestions. Let them think of the best way to get in touch with their referrals.

b) **The focus is not about helping you; it's about THEM helping OTHERS!**

   Remember: people refer you because they like to help people they care about and it makes them feel good to do so!

c) **The client takes responsibility and ownership of the process.**

   That is powerful! **They are committing to their idea rather than submitting to yours.** I would read that again.

This is not a sales conversation; it is a means to help other people leveraging the expertise of your client who will help if he or she knows, likes (Rule of Liking) and trusts you and has recognized your value (Rule of Reciprocation). And the power of the Rule of Commitment and Consistency (*see section 11 in this chapter*) works in your favor too:

d) **The question you ask EXPECTS a helpful response.**
Most of the time, your client will come up with something constructive not least because you expect an intelligent response.

e) **Your client might suggest bigger and more creative opportunities than what you would have asked for.**
Rather than just suggesting you call the other person, they might recommend that you speak at an industry-related event or that they introduce you to that prospect personally—you never know!

f) **If it doesn't work, it was their idea and your client is much more likely to suggest another.**

Should you get the response: "Well, I guess you could call them."

No referral system is perfect; there are too many intangibles in human relationships and how we communicate. If your client suggests you simply call the people you are asking about and you use your client's name when you call that prospect, you only have a 15% chance of doing business. So you want your client to warm it up to a 50% opportunity so that your call is expected (*see Chapter 1: 5-15-50-80*).

Here's what you say:

"Would you mind finding out if they'd be interested?"

When you say, "would you mind," people will not object. If they look slightly uncomfortable, it's because they don't know what to say to that person—that's what Step 5 is for.

The only other reason they will look uncomfortable is because they do not want to talk to the person in question—maybe they had a falling out recently or maybe they have not been in touch for a long time and it might be too weird to call out of the blue and say "Hey what kind of software do you guys use these days?"

In the rather unlikely event they want to know why you want the call warmed up, explain: "Otherwise it might feel to them like a cold call since they've never heard of me." Everybody hates being cold called so they will understand right away.

Should you get the response: *"Matt, I have no idea."*

This is the real world and sometimes your client will have no idea. **Then you will need to feed them some suggestions:**

- "I'd be happy to talk to your CEO/to do a brief presentation to your team over lunch/to join your department for its weekly meeting and introduce how I might be able to help them"

Or phrase them as questions:

- "Do you ever get together for lunch?"
- "Would it be easier to meet some of them at one of your weekly team meetings?" (People like the sound of the word "easy")
- "Would it possible for me to call her or shoot her an email?" or you could say
- "Well, what quite a lot of my clients have done is either set up a workshop in-house or they have asked me to stop by so that I could meet their CEO personally."

This approach leverages yet another Robert Cialdini universal principle of social influence, this one being 'social proof' which states that *we look to what others do to guide our behavior*. In other words, you suggest that everyone else is having you do a workshop or introducing you to the CEO, so it would be quite normal for them to do the same!

Example 3: Your client is a manger at a car plant that's doing some downsizing. These are all logical non-sales questions to ask:

a) *"I'm curious: are there other managers at your company in a similar situation to yours?*
b) *Now I have no idea if you guys ever talk about the financial decisions that need to be made (Step 4), but what would be the best way to find out if they might be interested in discussing some of this?*
c) *Would you mind finding out to see if they'd be interested in hearing from me some time?"*

This could lead to being introduced to a boss, other peers, a seminar opportunity, the HR director who doesn't understand the retirement options for their employees – sometimes something better that what you might have asked for.

Step 3: Now you have the name of someone else you can help! Congratulations! You can now move to step 5 (yes, Step 5 not Step 4).

DO IT! Practice is the only way you can get to be more successful with Step 3. The proof will be in the pudding because you will be helping your clients think of specific people.

• • •

7. Use Step 4: Reduce Their Resistance

> *"The self-image of the individual in the selling role traps him or her in a neediness mode and often leads to bad deals."*
>
> — Jim Camp, *Start With No*

The purpose to Step 4 is to weave into your Step 3 request that you do not expect your client to know the situation (need or interest level) of your referral request.

Hopefully you noticed the number of (Step 4's) in the previous two segments. You might want to re-read the previous segments again to see how Step 4 is used each time—always the same way.

It brings your request down to earth. It takes any awkwardness out of it. The edge of any neediness is removed: after all, you can't be 100% sure the person you're asking about has either a need or an interest; so you can sound more casual.

Here's your challenge: your client likes you, of course they know people—lots of them. However, each person has a unique situation, and your client certainly doesn't have all the details—especially as it relates to how you might help him.

If you just ask about the needs of somebody in the same life situation or line of work, your client's thoughts may go as follows: "Who'd benefit? My good friend Jeff might...yeah but I don't know what he does in this area. We don't really talk about it that much. And what would I say to him?" Their doubts start to kick in.

So it usually helps to acknowledge what they don't know, otherwise they might get uncomfortable bringing it up with someone important in their life:

Example 1: *"I don't expect you to know what his situation is. Obviously I don't either at this point. What would be the best way to find out if he might be interested?"*

Here's how it all moves together:

1. Finish up Step 2, the value conversation
2. *Then* you get specific, Step 3: *their parents*
3. Now you use Step 4 and reduce their resistance: you explain to your client that he may not know about his parents' situation
4. Maybe you tell a quick story that shows you empathize
5. *Then you* ASK!

Example 2:

1. *"Mark, I am really pleased this has been so helpful for you.*
2. *I know you mentioned your parents live nearby and that you saw them this weekend for your cousin's birthday.*
3. *I don't know if you've ever talked to them about what kind of planning they've done. (?)*
4. *I know before I got into this business, I never talked to my mother about this kind of stuff. I do remember though how glad I was when I found someone who I could recommend to her just so at least I had the peace of mind she was doing the right thing. I didn't want to stick my nose in her affairs. I was simply saying: I just want to make sure you're taken care of.*
5. *Do you know what your parents are doing with their estate planning? (Do you think they might be open to a quick conversation with me about some of that?) What do you think would be the best way to find out?"*

You may find this the hardest step to understand and master at first, but there will be times when it makes all the difference. There is something subtle yet effective about it.

Understanding Step 4 helps explain why the once recommended use of the question "who do you know who…" usually does not work. Your client does not know whether your referral request has a need or an interest so they honestly reply "I can't think of anyone right now," and you get no referrals. Even if the memory jogging produces a name, the name you get is still pretty cold because no need or interest is determined. Remember, it's just a "15%er."

Example 3: Try Humor!

Sometimes it pays to make a joke about how nobody talks about your line of work to others by suggesting that normal people talk about it all the time. What's effective about this approach is it can reduce someone's resistance to bringing it up in conversation.

One insurance agent client once told me that she had said to a customer: "I know you and your brothers are getting together for the Packer game this weekend. I expect when you guys hang out, you probably don't drink beer or watch the game much but you spend most of the time comparing the deductibles on your homeowners and auto policies, right?"

This got her a slightly dumbfounded look until she started laughing. Then he started laughing too at how ridiculous her comment was. While still in this feel-good moment, she said:

"I'm sure they both have insurance (Step 4—no need or interest assumed), but do you think they might be open to hearing from me to see if I could help them if you said something nice about me?"

So that Sunday he told his brothers that he had a new insurance agent who was "really nice and had a great sense of humor" and, since that did not describe their insurance provider, they both met with her and became customers too.

There are a couple of other areas where you may need to reduce the resistance of some clients on occasion:

a) Once in a while, your client will want to be reassured that everything you've talked about will remain confidential before they refer you.

b) Very occasionally people want to know how you follow up with referrals. Maybe they once had a bad experience after referring someone and they just need to hear that you won't be calling their good friend every day!

Only cross these bridges if you seem to run into them a fair bit. Really all you can do is to be aware of these concerns. As your confidence grows and you know your client is happy, you are more likely to inquire if you sense push-back from her. That's when you may find out that one of the above concerns needs to be addressed so you can reassure her and reduce any resistance.

DO IT! Start to work in a comment about how you don't expect your client to know about the needs or interest of your referral request. Dare to be funny about it!

• • •

8. Use Step 5: Coach Your Client to Warm Up the Referral

The purpose of Step 5 is to make sure your client says the right thing to your referral request so that you have permission to get in touch.

You can also do everything right to this point and lose the opportunity because your client says the wrong thing.

Don't leave this to chance!

I was talking to someone in Minnesota not long ago about him referring me to the corporate training department of his company. It is often unwise to just "hope" that your referral source will do a masterful job of knowing what to say. Why should they? Their minds are focused on their own lives.

So I asked him what he planned to say to this person. It wasn't very compelling. I was surprised. This company is using one of my most effective referral strategies in its national training program. Yet, if it had been me receiving the call, *I* would not have been interested in meeting *me* if I had heard the way this contact of mine had worded it!

So I fairly hastily jumped in and suggested he add that I specialize in one thing: working with advisors in financial services on how to get more referrals. And I made sure he got permission for me to call him (Step 6). Otherwise I was going to be waiting for this referral request to call me: no thanks!

You must have had the experience where a client has agreed to tell someone about you and returned saying "they weren't interested." And if you ask them, "I'm curious... what did you tell them?" you will likely cringe when they share what was said. "I told them you wanted to call them about a retirement plan." "I told them my financial advisor wanted to meet them and they said they already had a guy." "I told them someone I knew wanted to call them about a job selling insurance."

Coaching your referral sources how to warm up the referral will improve that name and number to a 50% chance of doing business—remember?

I find this is the least discussed referral topic often because people don't realize where things collapse in the referral process. It is not enough to simply be specific about who you want to meet. You want to take that name from a 15% to a 50% likelihood it will end in business. **Leads are a dying business.** You want warmed up referrals and once you know how to get them, it's worth the extra work up front.

So there are three reasons to coach your referral sources:

1. You don't want them to mess it up when you've done everything else right.
2. Most people have no idea how to talk to others about what you do. You must teach them what to say and make it easy for them!
3. You want them to warm up your referral so your referral request is expecting your call.

Here's the key to Step 5:

The only key = ***keep it simple.*** Their only job is to open the door and say:

"Michelle is great. You've got to talk to her. I'll have her call you."

They do not need to explain anything about the work you've done. It's not their job and most people can't explain it well anyway. The more they talk, the more likely it is that the person they are referring will find an excuse or a flaw in their logic and decline.

It's your job to sell yourself once the door has been opened.

Example 1 of What to Coach Your Client.

This script is all you need to direct your client's conversation with the referral:

"That's great, Mary. I appreciate you recommending Jennifer. The easiest thing to tell her is that:

a. *You're very pleased with the work we've done;*
b. *You highly recommend that she at least have a conversation with me, and;*
c. *Is it okay if I give her a call sometime?"* (keep this vague)

This wording is very non-threatening and does not make you sound needy. Note the third part: that you are getting permission to call (Step 6) and not letting them simply pass on your business card leaving you no further course of action but to sit by your phone and stare at it until it rings!

If you specialize in a certain niche market, that's worth including in part a). If you are building a specialization, you could mention that, too. People would much rather work with a specialist than a jack of all trades:

Example 2 of What to Coach Your Client:

a) *You're very pleased with the work we've been doing and that I specialize in helping contractors/women in transition/morticians/B&B owners/people who do exactly what you do;*
b) *You highly recommend that she at least have a conversation with me, and;*
c) *Would it be okay if I gave her a call in the near future?"*

"Tell them that I work with a lot of people in the gay and lesbian community and that you've been really pleased with the progress you've made."

"Tell them I specialize in helping pharmacists/people who have just been downsized, etc."

Example 3 of What to Coach Your Client:

John is a client of mine who, in 20 years, never asked for referrals until we started working together. Last week he got eight quality referrals in three days. In four months of our work, the return on his investment so far is $42,000. Here's something he learned from a client of his who had referred him unsolicited business:

"Just say to your friend what another client of mine says: 'I don't know how happy you are with the person you're working with (Step 4), but John is wonderful! And find out if it's okay for me to call him."

Now, he may change the word "wonderful" depending on who he is talking with, but it is simple and it works.

An e-mail or a follow up thank-you note is helpful when coaching others how to refer you.

Most people do not know how to talk about what you do to others. Step 5 sometimes can be accomplished more effectively in writing. Why? Because having it in black and white can help people remember what to say about you. Anything that makes it easier for others to introduce you is a good thing! Not to mention that it makes it less likely they'll mess up their sincere efforts to help people they care about.

It also gives you an excuse to "assume" the referral by sending a gentle reminder and coach the referral source what to say:

Hi Dave,

Great meeting you today. Thanks again for talking to your manager to see if she'd be open to hearing from me.

All you need to tell her is that you've been very pleased with the work we've done; that you highly recommend that she at least have a quick conversation with me; and is it okay if I give her a call sometime?

I'll probably drop you a line in a couple of weeks. (Step 6) Hope your son's baseball tournament is fun this weekend!

--Matt

Here's a more business-specific example used by one of my clients (two business partners). Their assistant e-mails this to the referral source and asks her to use this wording in an email to the person being referred:

Hi Sarah,

Two of my business colleagues, Bryan Beauchamp and Sy Maleki, would welcome the opportunity to visit with you. They are co-owners of Beauchamp Maleki Consulting, and they specialize in Business Succession Planning, Executive Benefit Planning, and Non-Qualified Deferred Compensation. In addition to being well-connected networkers, they have done good work for my clients and I think it could be a good use of your time to visit with them. Would you be open to getting together for golf or a drink after work in the near future with Bryan and me? If so, please let us know what dates fit into your schedule.

Thanks!

Michelle

DO IT! Don't make the mistake of assuming your referral source has the gift of the gab. Get increasingly used to taking charge of teaching them what to say.

• • •

9. Use Step 6: Keep Control of the Process

The purpose of Step 6 is to make sure YOU always have permission to take action so that you can get an appointment with your referral request.

You can also do everything right to this point and lose the opportunity because you turn control over to your client by now needing to wait to hear from him or her to do something. Don't leave this to chance. Keep control of the process.

You always want to have permission to make the next call to your referral source. Don't just hand out a business card and ask them to pass it on. Don't just HOPE something will happen. Most people's businesses offer important but not urgent products and services.

Example: *"When should I get back to you to see if she's interested?"*

Why this works:

1. **It gets your clients to think about when they'll have that conversation.** Also, they will suggest an actual timeframe when you should call them back about it—often something like "why don't you call me in a couple of weeks?" That way, when you do follow up, you can simply say: "You'd suggested this would be a good time to get back to you. Did you get a chance to talk to Jonathan yet?" This is very non-threatening and makes you simply an obedient professional doing his or her job.

2. **Your client is taking responsibility and ownership for the solution, just like with "Ask the Expert."** It is their idea. So if they don't make the call when they say they will, they are much more likely to feel awkward about it because they have not kept their word. They will feel some internal inconsistency.

   Of course, this will happen. We're talking about human beings who are not perfect and have other priorities! That's why persistence is so important in asking for what you want. But, this process is the highest level of accountability you can get.

3. **It's not pushy.** It's not you saying: *"I tell you what: I'll call you on Monday at 9am. Shall I call you on your cell phone or your office line? Or would Tuesday at 2pm be better?"* Ouch! Avoid sounding needy.

There are two exceptions I can think of:

a) If there is a clear reason that timing matters. Perhaps you have an event deadline or a special offer that expires at a certain time. Then you might say: *"I'd really like to connect with you before the end of the month and I'm going to be gone on vacation the week of the 24th. Is it okay if I get back to you around the 19th?"*

b) If they tell you they will see someone on Friday or over the weekend, it makes more sense to say: *"Okay, well how about I drop you a line early next week then?"*

DO IT! And do not change the wording of this question. It works really well exactly as it is.

• • •

10. Know How to Handle Objections

Q: How do you handle someone who says they can think of someone but want to talk to him/her first?

If they want to warm up the referral to make sure it's a good fit, praise the person and coach them properly so that they say the right thing. That's Step 5.

If they won't mention the person's name and they are being cagey with you, it's because they are worried about how you will follow-up with someone who is pretty important to them. And maybe they don't really want their name involved. This is a bad sign.

You are most likely hearing this because the person is not really impressed, and you have not really added enough value.

Or they have had bad personal experiences with someone hounding a referral they once gave and they need reassurance on this (*see Step 4*).

Here are some suggestions for those who say they have someone in mind but are less forthcoming:

You: *That's great you have someone in mind and I totally understand you wanting to check with them first. I'm the same way.*

{pause}

(try to find out if this person is a qualified referral)
As you know, the people I can help the most are ex. Companies that lease a lot of cars; what does this person do for a living?

(They respond)

Okay, sure, that's great.

You: *What many of my clients have found is the EASIEST thing to say is something like:*
"Greg's a great guy, he's helped my company out a lot and I just think you should talk to him."
And then ask: *"Is it okay if he gives you a call sometime in the near future?"*

(Now you want to help them identify a plan in their mind to ask this person before they get in their car, listen to their voice messages, turn on the radio and get too busy again!)

THEN ask:
You: *What have you found is the best way to get a hold of this person?*
(They'll tell you.)

{pause}

Thanks again for doing that. That's great. When should I drop you a line to find out if he's interested?"

Q. How do you handle "I've already to talked to them about you" and you haven't heard anything?

You: *"What did you tell them?"*

Most of the time their response will explain why nobody rushed to the phone to call you! Return to Step 5 and coach them properly.

You: *I appreciate you saying something. I think that because what I do is very important but rarely urgent, most people procrastinate on getting in touch with me* (this lets them off the hook without making them look/feel bad).

> *If you wouldn't mind just mentioning my name one more time; sometimes it's easier to just say: "Kathy specializes in xyz—she does a very detailed analysis. She really is worth a quick conversation with and she's super nice. Would you mind her calling you some time?"*

Q. How do you handle: "I gave them your card" and nothing happens?

Exactly the same as the last answer!

Q. How do you handle: "They said they were already working with someone"?

This one is more complicated because it depends on how happy that person is with their current provider and how enthusiastically you were endorsed. If someone is on the fence with where they currently do business, a strong endorsement can go a long way to having them consider hearing from you. Sometimes they need repeat requests or to be invited to meet you in a non-threatening environment.

If you run into this quite often, your best bet is to address it with your clients before they ask.

> *"I'm sure your friend Margie already has financing with another bank. However, perhaps you could share that the reason people work with me is because:*
> *Benefit A*
> *Benefit B*
> *Benefit C*
>
> *And see if she'd be open to hearing from me some time?"*

I recall a recent meeting I had with an estate planning attorney and a financial advisor who were grappling with this. A specific example was being discussed about a client who already had a relationship with an advisor.

My point was that:

a) The original advisor did not specialize in working with privately-held companies worth between $10-100 million.

b) Not all people with same job title are created equally! Were all the teachers you had at school equally effective instructors? Would you ask most third grade teachers to evaluate and edit the content of a Ph.D. dissertation? If the original advisor were that competent, he or she would not have recommended the current (inappropriate) insurance coverage to begin with.

c) Robert Cialdini's Rule of Authority states that we look to experts to show us the way, so the attorney's enthusiastic recommendation of this other advisor would make a big difference!

• • •

11. Why Steps 3, 5, and 6 Work So Well: The Rule of Commitment and Consistency.

> *"It is, quite simply, our nearly obsessive desire to be (and to appear) consistent with what we have already done."*
>
> — Robert Cialdini, *Influence*

Here's why it's so important to leverage as much of your client's expertise as possible in identifying the referral, warming up the referral, and advising you on how to follow-up.

The more I study Robert Cialdini's research on social influence, the more I learn about what's effective in getting referrals (both the right and the wrong way). The importance of asking your client for advice on the best way to be referred (Steps 3, 5, and 6 of the 6 Steps) is underlined by his research and by one of his six universal principles of social influence: The Rule of Commitment and Consistency.

The Power of Your Clients Making a Commitment to Refer You

In a referral conversation, you want your client to commit to their idea (how they think you should contact someone) rather than submit to yours ("can you give me their information and tell them I'll be calling?").

Fully understanding the principle that how committed your clients are to THEIR IDEAS and to keeping their word can go a long way to helping you get higher quality and more warmed-up referrals. It's remarkable!

The more your clients believe that the referral was their idea rather than yours, the more committed they will be in following up on it. This is why the Ask the Expert approach to getting referrals is so effective *("what would be the best way to find out if Sally might be interested?"* or *"how would you recommend I find out if other partners at your firm might get similar value?")*.

Cialdini has found that we are most committed to something that we believe was our decision, and that we took responsibility for it and did so with no outside pressure (such as being offered a reward or gift—or with your kids it might be a bribe or threat so that they comply to behave).

Other factors that increase your commitment and your client's commitment to following through include:

a) **Declaring it in public:** Having your client say out loud what she intends to do to contact a referral can go a long way to making sure you get an opportunity to help that person or that group.

b) **Writing it down:** Perhaps gently reminding a client about information he gave you in writing or put in an e-mail will help nudge him along to follow-through. You might bring up THEIR idea by saying: *"I'm just following up on something you mentioned in an e-mail you sent to me on the 16th. You put something about how I* *might want to contact your friend Pauline Jefferson. What would you recommend I do there?"*

This is why you've heard so many people endorse writing down your goals. It's been proven to help you achieve them because your commitment increases!

c) **The harder it is to attain something, the more committed you are to it and the more you value it.** This can be anything in life, from pursuing your dream partner and then finding the commitment a no-brainer to training for a marathon and then staying in excellent health. Boot camp in the Marines is so brutal that people emerge "more resilient, simply braver, and better for the wear." Why do you think you see so many Marines bumper stickers on cars? A tough life experience can make people more loyal and persistent.

This is likely another reason why persistence with a prospect pays and why so much business is done because we persist. It was hard to attain and the bond is therefore stronger.

Finally, this is why some companies and industries find it is worthwhile to bring on new clients by having them make a small purchase. This foot-in-the-door technique works because it leverages the commitment now made. It's why many insurance companies are happy to have you start out buying just car insurance. Once you're a customer, it is easier then to discuss other products and services. It's similar with banks starting you out with checking accounts.

Inconsistency is an undesirable personality trait.

One of the key motivators behind our behavior is the need and pressure we feel to be seen as consistent. **So if your client tells you that she will follow up with a referral and she said it sincerely, she will feel awkward about not keeping her word—about looking inconsistent. Knowing this can help you persist in following up.**

She gave you her word!

The power of us wanting to be seen as consistent with our word was tested by psychologist Thomas Moriarty on New York City beaches and written about in Cialdini's book, *Influence*. His task was to find out to what extent people would take their verbal commitment—even if it meant stopping a crime. Here's how his experiment went:

The first time, Person A would find a spot on the beach, lay out a towel and lounge there for a while listening to his radio. Then he would leave those things behind and shortly after Person B would grab the radio and hurry off. Only four people in twenty challenged the thief.

The second time a slight twist was added. Person A did the same things, but before leaving would ask someone nearby to "watch his things." Person B came along and stole the radio but that was when the unsuspecting watcher turned into a virtual vigilante. 19 of the 20 chased the thief and some even physically restrained the person or snatched the radio away!

In that instance, there was some danger that people were prepared to face in order to look consistent. Have you ever been asked to watch someone's stuff? I remember feeling that level of responsibility at a large book shop once when asked to keep an eye on a mother's possessions because she needed to take her young daughter to a different floor to use the restroom.

The scary part is we will also act against our own best interests to maintain being seen as consistent.

I used to take these step aerobic classes at my gym partly in the hopes of meeting eligible women there. Many people who went had their favorite spot to set up their steps, and mine was always in the front row on the right. After some time, I started noticing an attractive dark-haired woman who always would set up in the back row on the left of the gym—a distance I would have no logical reason to stray during pauses in the workout if I wanted to get to know her a little (I later found out she was engaged).

So the next time I went, I set up my steps on the back left row trying to convince myself "it's good not to always do the same thing." But other people noticed immediately and said to me: "Matt! What are doing back there? Why aren't you up front like you usually are?" I actually blushed out of embarrassment because I was being seen as inconsistent. I mumbled something feeble like "Oh, I just felt like a change." I felt like I might as well have put up a big sign saying: "Hey Everyone! I'm only back here to hit on this dark-haired woman!" It was almost ridiculous how much it rocked the status quo. So the next time I took the class I returned to the front right row. Being seen as flighty was too painful!

So remember: Fully understanding the principle that how committed your clients are to THEIR IDEAS and to keeping their word can go a long way to helping you get higher quality and more warmed-up referrals.

The more your clients believe that the referral was their idea rather than yours, the more committed they will be in following up on it.

CHAPTER 7:

Fearless Referral Follow-Up

1. Keep your referral sources happy and updated.

This is one area in which the vast majority of people do a HORRIBLE job. Very rarely do people keep their referral sources informed about what happened to their referrals. I understand that it can take a long time between getting the referral and actually meeting that person, but remember that people's integrity is on the line. It is very possible that people who have referred you in the past have stopped because they felt unappreciated since they never heard from you!

I recommend some kind of reminder system or weekly habit to check in and see that your referral sources have been contacted recently. Often they will go to bat for you again!

E-mail is great for updating referral sources.

I hardly ever hear about referrals I give to others, and I used to be very weak at keeping others informed as to what had happened to their referrals.

I understand that it's difficult—especially when business can take months to develop and phone tag can get frustrating. But we truly do forget that someone once cared enough to refer us, and we owe it to them to keep in touch. If he or she has sent the implicit message that they know, like, and trust us enough to refer us, we should be going out of our way to build that relationship. There could easily be more referrals in the future from this person.

Also, a greatly under-utilized way to get stubborn referrals to call us back to is to send e-mails like this to your referral source:

Hi Michelle.

Hope life is good. Just wanted to update you that I have left three messages for your brother over the past 6 weeks and have not heard back yet.

Any suggestions?

Best of luck with your seminar next week!

Matt

Most of the time in this instance, I find that "Michelle" will feel badly that her referral has not bothered to call me and she will often respond saying that she will nudge him along or she may have a good explanation as to why I've heard nothing (perhaps their mother has been sick).

This can work well by phone but I think is more effective in an e-mail if it's really all I have to say to this person. I often prefer not to interrupt someone's day just to tell them this. The telephone can be better if you have other things to call about that are adding value to the other person, and if your tone of voice is very patient and casual like it's no big deal that you've haven't heard back yet. If you feel even slightly irritated, stick to e-mail where hopefully they can't sense your frustration or disappointment!

And the only solution I know of to keep referral sources well informed is to make it a weekly habit as you go through your prospect file.

1. Thank your referral source

2. Build and mine this relationship on purpose!

• • •

2. A Simple System for Keeping Track of Your Referrals

Once you start getting referrals, congratulations! Now you will likely start running into a new challenge—not getting all your calls returned.

Once common question I hear running seminars is: "What do I do once I have referrals?"

You Only Prospect Twice: when you feel like it and when you don't.

1) You want **one location** with the following info: their contact info, name of referral source, each date of contact (minimum of 5 - persistence), room for personal comments, and the end result. You want to have physical space in your system to write personal comments, such as "call in a month: just had a baby" or "ask about their vacation to Mexico."

   This is so prospects don't fall through the cracks.

2) You schedule time to review your prospect list **at least weekly.** This must happen (*see section 6 in this chapter*).

3) You keep referral sources informed as to how things are progressing (*see section 1*).

4) Sometimes you also need to think of other creative ways to get your name in front of prospects when your voice mail messages aren't working. Answer the question for that person: How else can I add value to this person?

   I usually prospect sales managers so several years ago I realized I needed to ask myself: What is important to them? What would help them in their jobs? What should I read more of that has ideas that they would appreciate? What events in their community do I know of that they should know about and might not?

Two Keys for Effective Follow-Up Calls:

Key One: Never sound needy.

In Jim Camp's book, *Start With No*, he reminds us how important it is not to sound needy—like your calling them is doing them a favor and that you really don't need the business. One suggestion he makes is to tell people:

a) how much you would like to meet them, and
b) (if this is true) that you are not sure if they're interested,
c) they should let you know either way.

This way you sound professional, interested, and not desperate—that it won't impact your livelihood (you are already doing well and if you're not, act the part in advance!). He argues that this relaxes your prospects, and I have found that more people get back to me sooner, usually to say that they are still interested. And if they're not, wouldn't you rather know?

A few weeks ago over a stout at a microbrewery, a financial advisor having his best year ever said to me that if he wasn't hearing people say no, he wasn't talking to enough people. That's an empowering mindset because this is the real world.

Key Two: Use the word "because."

Robert Cialdini's research has found that even when we don't have a very good reason, humans respond remarkably more positively when we give them a reason using the word "because."

Here is a sample script:

"Hi Steve, this is Matt Anderson.

DAVE HARPER recommended I get in touch with you.

I'm not sure how much he explained to you about what I do;

I have been helping him (for example) map out a retirement plan.

(Tip #1) Dave wasn't sure about your situation and I don't know either. Maybe you have no interest in a brief conversation. If not, just tell me. That's fine.

(Tip #2) But he did recommend us meeting because he's been very pleased with what we've accomplished so far.

I was wondering if we could set up a brief meeting/quick cup of coffee/grab a quick lunch and connect on how your financial goals are coming along and see if there's a fit with how I help/work with business owners like Dave/young families/retirees/other dentists.

If you could call or e-mail me with two or three times that work for you, either leave me a message at (608) 843-3827 or shoot me an e-mail to Matt@TheReferralAuthority.com

Thanks and I'll look forward to talking to you soon."

Three Tips for More Success Following Up:

Tip One: Zig Ziglar has a story about meeting with parents who can't control their kids. He says that if these people cannot say no to their kids, this is a sure sign of prospects that will have a hard time saying no to you. He also says the same for people who do not cancel appointments but don't show up. If they don't have the backbone to even call and say "no thanks," they are likely going to have a hard time telling you no when you decide to get in front of them.

Tip Two: Most people admire those who persist—especially other business people. Your persistence makes a statement that you believe in why you are calling, and the other person's resistance often drops. It does seem that many people's mindset has shifted to one that says "I won't call them back. If they are really keen to talk they can call me again." The etiquette is simply to leave polite messages each time and call as if it's the first time you've left a message. I really believe it is the tone of our voices that makes a big difference. Sometimes I will mention a date we talked or met so I come across as professional and organized (and to politely remind the person that it has been a while!).

Tip Three: If you are uncomfortable calling people, find the best time and place for YOU to make your calls. Certainly after a sale is always an easier time to call. For me, it was a long time before I realized I most enjoyed calling people when I was driving somewhere. I felt like I had more of a sense of mission when I was calling on the road, like it was the only time I could call them. There were also times when I enjoyed calling people from a favorite café with a favorite beverage in front of me. This felt more like fun.

• • •

3. What to Say When You Follow Up on Your Referrals.

Here's the scenario: your happy client, Jennifer, has referred you to Brian, who is a great prospect. If it's a quality referral, and Brian has given permission for you to contact him. In other words, it's a warmed up referral which means that 50% of the time it should lead to business. Clearly you don't want to drop the ball, but you're busy, right?

What do you do next?

1. **CALL Brian.**

Only e-mail him if Jennifer has told you that that's the best way to contact him. E-mails are too easy to ignore.

If Brian answers the phone:

(Please note: in all the sample scripts EVERY sentence is there for a very good reason, either to reduce the other person's resistance to meeting or to make sure you don't sound needy in any way.)

> *"Hi Brian, this is Matt Anderson calling from the Referral Authority. Jennifer Davies put us in touch a few days ago and said that you might be interested in a quick conversation about ways I might be able to help you/your business. Am I catching you at a good time?"*

The goal here is to get an appointment on the calendar if Brian is a good prospect for you. So if you need to determine that first, you will ask a few extra questions.

Most of the time, we have to leave Brian a voice message:

> *"Hi Brian, this is Matt Anderson calling from the Referral Authority. Jennifer Davies forwarded your contact information to me suggesting you might be interested in a quick conversation about ways I might be able to help you/your business.* ***She wasn't sure if you would be interested*** *but she did want to connect us* ***because*** *she has been really pleased with the results she has gotten from the work she's done with me. The best time*

to catch me this week is on Thursday morning before noon or next Monday afternoon. Please let me know when would be a good time to reach you in the next 2-3 weeks."

2. **If you are currently dropping the ball following up, leave the first message yourself and indicate who will be following up instead of you until the appointment is set.**

"Hi Brian, this is Matt Anderson calling from the Referral Authority. Jennifer Davies gave me your contact information and said she had talked to you recently about the work that we've done and that you might be interested in getting together some time. Obviously I'm not sure what your situation is and whether there's a fit or not, but perhaps we can find a time to figure that out. You're welcome to try calling me at (608) 843-3827. My assistant, Susie, manages my schedule, so she would be the best person to call unless you have questions for me. Please drop her a line at (608) 831-0510 or I'll ask her to follow up with you in the next couple of weeks."

When your assistant starts the follow up calls, here are a couple of versions making sure NEVER to sound irritated that calls are not being returned and in fact to have the tone of your voice sound like you are calling for the first time!

"Hi Brian, this is Susie Switzer calling from Matt Anderson's office. ***Jennifer Davies*** *connected the two of you a couple of weeks ago. I am following up on Matt's behalf* ***because*** *Jennifer had recommended that you both at least have a conversation some time. I was just calling to see what might work for you in the next 2-3 weeks. If you could let me know, that would be much appreciated. My number is (608) 831-0510. I hope your day's going well and I look forward to talking to you soon."*

"Hi Brian, this is Susie Switzer calling from Matt Anderson's office. Matt asked me to drop you a line because back in April you had expressed some interest to Jennifer Davies that you might be interested in having a brief conversation with him some time about bringing in more referral business. I don't know if you're still interested or not and I certainly don't want to keep calling you if you're not (!), but it would be great to hear from you one way or the other. Jennifer has been very pleased with the results she has gotten working with Matt, and we certainly wouldn't be following up

if we thought it would likely be a waste of your time. Please let me know about putting something on the calendar or what you like us to do next—if anything! My number is (608) 831-0510. Thanks, and hopefully we can connect in the near future!"

3. **Create a tracking system so that at least five follow-up calls or e-mails are made**

Remember the study of persistence in sales that found that 94% of people give up before asking five times for the business, yet 60% of business is closed after we ask five times? Most people call once or twice and give up if they don't hear anything.

If you would like to use the referral tracking system I use, I've included it at the back of this book!

4. **Spread out your follow-up calls**

I can't say there's a magic wait time between calls. I used to almost always wait two weeks between calls, but sometimes that's a mistake as we need to strike while the iron is hot. In other instances, people aren't ready to decide or something comes up in their life that is far more important than what we do and we have to accept that and ask them: "what would you like me to do next?" or "when would you like me to follow back up?"

Alternatively we also need to identify the difference between important and urgent for our prospects sometimes. Many people live a lifestyle now where they see urgency and busyness everywhere, and your job may be to step in and suggest that procrastination may not be wise.

5. **Instill an empowering mindset about following-up with prospects.**

The most helpful mindset is to remind yourself that most people admire tenacity because they don't have it! It also helps to remind yourself that some people will hear your messages and say things to themselves along the lines of: "Wow. This person really wants my business. They must be pretty confident they can help me. They seem to want to work with me a lot more than the company I currently use."

6. **Honor your referral source.**

Thank your referral sources and keep them informed. This one point alone is a grossly underutilized strategy to get more referrals. Why do we usually do such a poor job of nurturing our relationship with that person? It's not like there's an unending number of people telling the world about us!

Everyone likes to be appreciated (at least thanked), and sometimes rewarded. Rewards are effective when they are unexpected and personally meaningful to that individual. Last week a client on a group referral coaching call of mine said he had given a referral source a $25 gift card to Menards (DIY store). For me that would be about as exciting as getting a magazine on knitting but when I asked him why he'd chosen that store, he shared that this gift had gone down extremely well because this was the person's favorite place to shop. Perfect!

You must have a system in place for tracking referrals and referral sources. Remember that you must schedule time to review this list weekly. It's not hard to do and will produce terrific long-term benefits.

THE BEST COMPLIMENT I CAN RECEIVE IS A REFERRAL TO YOUR FRIENDS, FAMILY, OR BUSINESS ASSOCIATES!
Goodfellas' Business Solutions, LLC
KIRK

4. Mastering the Big Picture Where Referrals Fit In: Goals and Habits

> *"You have exactly as much time as the richest person in the world, the most powerful person, and the wisest person: 24 hours each day."*
>
> — Dan Baker

> *"Self-discipline is the ability to make yourself do what you should do, when you should do it, whether you feel like it or not."*
>
> — Elbert Hubbard

The big picture to your referral business is the rest of your life and where it all fits in. There is definitely a time and a place to step back and make sure you are heading in the right direction.

I am compelled to share the time management system I've been using for over 15 years because so many people blame lack of time as a major impediment in their life. Just last week (at the time I was writing this), a client of mine complained for the umpteenth time that he just never had enough time in his life and—for our purposes—to follow up effectively with the referrals he was working so hard to get in the first place! I offered him some short-term suggestions, but it really starts at the top with being ever clearer about what you want in life.

"The mantra of the millennium is 'I don't have time. I don't have time. I don't have time.'" Dan Baker, in his wonderful book *What Happy People Know*, expresses no sympathy for this so-called belief, pointing out that **there are still 24 hours in every day. He argues that we are programmed by fear to want everything often because we feel like we are not good enough as we are.**

> *"The real culprit is making decisions that are driven by fear: choosing too much, choosing a happiness trap* as a priority, or not choosing at all. These are actions that squander time and render it scarce."*

(*The happiness traps are worth listing: trying to buy happiness; trying to find it through pleasure/indulgence; trying to over-analyze the past and end up a victim; trying to overcome weaknesses; trying to force happiness)

His advice is to make sure you prioritize what is truly most valuable to you. The three areas that fulfill us most are our purpose, our health, and our relationships. This leads me back to the Big Picture.

Goals: This is a great place to start. There are many excellent books on this topic. My favorites are Brian Tracy's book, *Goals!,* David Rock's book, *Personal Best,* Fiona Harrold's book, *Be Your Own Life Coach,* and Stephen Covey's classic book, *The 7 Habits of Highly Effective People.* David Rock gets you to have some fun creating short and snappily-worded goals that really resonate with you. At present I like starting my day out with Brian Tracy's method of writing out 12 month goals in the present tense and starting each sentence with the word "I." For example, I earn $x, I work out x times/week, I enjoy time with my family x times/year etc. This is fun so long as you stretch yourself and think bigger with your goals or else it can get monotonous. The real juice comes from picturing each one actually existing in your life.

I also enjoy John Eliot's contrarian perspective in *Overachievement* that goals can be limiting if you want to be a high achiever. His research with peak performers at Rice University finds that you can get too focused on detail and strategies rather than passionately pursuing the dream, enjoying and excelling at the process and focusing on what's possible.

The real point here is to create something big that you're up to. Goals based around what matters most to you can get you excited and in action. Remember: it's what they make of you not what they make for you that counts. Your business and financial goals can all be impacted significantly by getting consistently more high quality referrals. That's why you're reading this!

Habits: Many of us try out new ideas and strategies in our business, and even though we see some positive results we do not turn them into habits. There are things we did when we first started out that helped us get where we are today—and yet we stopped doing them!

Whether it was because those activities were always outside our comfort zone or because they required greater self-discipline, the fact is we are living small, avoiding complete responsibility, and not fulfilling our potential by avoiding doing these important and effective things.

The book that has influenced me more than any other has to be Stephen Covey's *The 7 Habits of Highly Effective People*. This is information that the growing Gen Y may not be as familiar with. Please spread the word so that they recognize the timeless power of these seven habits:

1. **Be proactive:** Take complete responsibility for all areas of your life—this is much easier said than done. How's your health? Is there something more you could be doing there? What about your financial situation? Relationships with family members? It's very easy to put the blame "out there" but this resolves nothing.

2. **Begin with the end in mind:** Know where you want to go in all areas of your life. When Alice tells the Cheshire Cat in *Alice in Wonderland* that she doesn't know where she wants to go, the cat replies: "Well, then, any road will do." Don't be another Alice!

3. **Put first things first:** Not pursuing the most important things in life is the cause of most of our unhappiness. You want to spend your time on the first things in your life.

4. **Think Win/Win:** Life and business work so much better when both parties are happy. This is why I believe that asking for and getting referrals should strengthen relationships. Your job is to make sure that the person who referred you is going to get a thank you and great feedback. Your goal is to make that referral source feel terrific—not least so they will refer you again but also to honor the relationships that are being impacted. Everybody has put their integrity on the line.

   How can you grow a business if you're squeezing referrals out of people who are not particularly impressed with the work you've done? It violates every principle out there. That's why you want to ask clients to tell you about the value they have received.

5. **Seek first to understand, then to be understood:** poor communication is the main reason for challenges in life and business. Make sure the other person knows he or she has been understood before you respond. Much easier said than done! For most of us this is a skill to develop.

6. **Synergize:** you cannot get to the top on your own no matter how proud you are about being "independent." Reaching out for support and guidance and working together with others will move you from good to great. If you are obsessed with doing it all yourself, you are not at the top of your game. I know not least because that's how I used to be!

7. **Sharpen the Saw:** this means that if you don't take care of yourself first, you are no good to anyone. You have physical, emotional, spiritual, and mental needs that must all be nurtured and kept active for you to be an effective person.

DO IT! Start with the Brian Tracy approach to setting 12 month goals in the present tense.

Goals and habits are the first piece to mastering your time and deciding where the referrals you want come into play. There is a second more strategic piece and that's weekly planning.

• • •

5. Finding the Time for Your Goals, Habits, and Referral Asking: Weekly Planning

> *"The week becomes the "normal lens" that gives the most accurate perspective for creating a balanced quality life."*
>
> — Stephen Covey, *First Things First*

Weekly planning allows you to turn your goals into habitual actions and strategies so that you do put your first things first and stay on top of the referral strategies that grow your business.

Daily planning is too reactive on its own; it focuses too closely on the urgent rather than the important (although I highly recommend Andrew Carnegie's strategy of identifying the top six things each day and starting with the first one until it is complete. He attributed much of his success to this one daily habit). These are strategies I learned mostly from Stephen Covey's *First Things First* and have personalized over the last 15 years.

First review your goals.

Second, identify your roles in life: spouse, father, daughter, friend, career, volunteer, board member etc. It is best to have no more than seven roles.

Third, decide what you want to do this week—you do not have to fill every role every week. That will depend on your first things! Put these things on your schedule first. Covey calls them the "big rocks" that you prioritize by making sure they go on your schedule first not so that you can pack more into your week but rather to make sure that they get prioritized.

Then you make room for your next layer of activities. I have developed a list of more than 30 habits that I go through each week. I pause and consider what I am doing in that area and schedule whatever I need to that relates to that area. It helps me enormously in making sure I put in the big rocks first and that I do not overlook practices that have helped get me to where I am.

My list used to be a few things and it used to take me 20 minutes. But I have found it so useful that every time I realize there is something that I cannot afford to forget, it becomes a weekly habit. I recognize it's very detail-oriented, but the benefits far outweigh the time it takes to plan and I always feel a certain peace of mind when I'm done, that I have a good handle on what's coming up. You will too.

Here is my current list of habits. Some serve primarily as important reminders:

1. Review and update goals
2. Schedule workouts
3. Friends and family time, dates
4. Pay myself first, make tax payments, pay bills, balance books
5. Assignments from my coach
6. Writing time
7. Prospecting time and review of primary business card collection
8. Client prep time
9. Presentation prep time
10. Product making time (CDs, DVDs, manuals)
11. Pre-plan asks/referral requests for the week (*see Chapter* 4)
12. Meeting confirmation reminders
13. Loyalty Ezine writing time
14. Networking time
15. Prepare task list for Assistant
16. Update referral sources on referrals received
17. Personal and professional development (classes, reading, workshops)
18. Professional volunteer commitments (committees, boards)
19. Update managers about groups I'm working with
20. Add value to prospects/key people
21. LinkedIn time
22. Personal volunteer commitments (kids improv comedy coaching)
23. Hikes/time in nature
24. Fiction/movie/sports watching time
25. Birthday list
26. Holiday savings
27. Profit and loss review with bookkeeper
28. Supplies inventory (paper, ink cartridges etc.)
29. Household maintenance/cleaning
30. Groceries
31. Ironing/dry cleaning
32. Car maintenance
33. Pet care
34. Weekly review

Clearly, you will want to prioritize your own list and add/delete as appropriate. More than anything this planning helps to keep you in a proactive mode as often as possible taking care of things so that there are many fewer breakdowns and last-minute stressors.

The last item, the weekly review, can be very valuable. It takes seconds to skim over each of the past seven days and evaluate what you did at a glance and it's a great way to be clear on how valuable each meeting you had was. Five years ago I was in seven different organizations to network. Needless to say they were not all created equally in terms of helping me grow my business. This quick survey helped me identify quicker where to spend more time. This review is also helpful for one-on-one meetings. There are plenty of nice people out there to have coffee with but how much do they all impact your business and network?

DO IT! I know this might look like a time-consuming task but I assure you that planning ahead in these areas makes life much less stressful and, ultimately, frees up time to do more of what you want.

• • •

6. The Team You Need to Get You to the Top

> *"The overwhelming majority of the most successful people on earth rely on advice, support, encouragement, and forceful nudging from a few trusted people who help them when they stumble, falter, or waver."*
>
> — Keith Ferrazzi, *Who's Got Your Back*

Now you've got all the information you need to get comfortable asking for referrals and you know when to ask and what to say, will you do it? The odds suggest you may not.

Here's the challenge: We are a culture of do-it-yourselfers. Most people think they can do everything on their own—especially once they think they know more-or-less how. They believe that it is weak to reach out for help and support and that this would make them no longer look good—which is a pretty deep-seated fear of ours!

I used to be one of those people. I worked alone, lived alone, and was 4,000 miles from my family. My favorite personal development book was *Be Your Own Life Coach*, my favorite health book was *Treat Your Own Back* (see a theme here?!) Even though my favorite business book was *The 7 Habits of Highly Effective People*, I somehow managed never to apply habit 6—synergize with others and be interdependent! I continued trying to do everything myself. And it kept me small. My only solution was to read more books and work harder. I love reading, but books are not enough.

What you do is all that matters. And none of us are islands. You must have a support team!

Napoleon Hill wrote about one solution in his 1937 classic, *Think and Grow Rich*. He devoted an entire chapter to the importance of the mastermind group and declared that nobody can "have great power" without it! Benefit from the experience, intelligence and insights of others. You cannot live long enough to figure everything out yourself. And such a group can help sustain your positive emotions.

In Keith Ferrazzi's second book, *Who's Got Your Back*, he writes about developing "lifeline relationships"—which he defines as a small team of individual advisors who give you **feedback, coaching, accountability and support** to make certain that you flourish.

These four things are what you need to become accomplished at getting high quality referrals on a consistent basis. This is why top performers (and athletes and performers) hire coaches.

Why would you want such a team of advisors?

1. To go from good to great!

First, look at the evidence. In Chapter 1 I wrote about deliberate practice and the fact that almost no one gets to the top without coaching. All the best professional athletes and performers work with coaches. You know this and expect it, although you don't stop to ask why they do and you don't! The problem is you don't think you should get the same, partly because you are not on a multi-million dollar contract with a pro team or recording company. You make the assumption somehow that it's just for "them"—the superstar super humans.

But wait! In 2008, Russ Alan Prince's book *The Middle Class Millionaire* revealed that most of the people he studied with a net worth between $2-$15 million *did the same thing!* These are not well-known people—just people who have learned from the best. It's time for you to do the same. They are individuals who did not balk at hiring business coaches and consultants to help them in areas that they needed help to go from good to great. These millionaires knew they were not experts at everything, and they realized they did not have the time to be experts at everything. No one does.

They also hired the best legal and accounting help. They hired the top advisors for financial and real estate consulting. Many hired personal trainers—not necessarily because they were out of shape, but for the four coaching benefits highlighted above.

So it's not just the knowledge! It's finding people who will hold you accountable and point out your blind spots so that you can live a bigger life and fulfill your potential.

2. Your advisors will help you create your own definition of success and will help you develop a plan to get there.

3. The team will help you figure out what you need to STOP doing to get there.

4. It will provide ongoing support to sustain change (and keep you OUT of your comfort zone).

How do you make these relationships work for you? The four reasons to pursue these relationships are so you end up reaching your goals—whether that's getting more referrals or something else:

1. Support

You need people cheering you on—especially those who have no ulterior motive but to see you succeed. Nothing can be more detrimental than key people in your life doubting you at every turn. Reach out to others and ask for more help!

To be effectively supported, Ferrazzi believes that ***"the secret ingredient to establish genuine lifeline relationships is vulnerability."*** When you disclose what's really important and talk about your challenges, people can relate to you better—it is likely they have been there too!

2. A personal trainer for your business life

Even when we are doing well enough, it never hurts to have someone push us further knowing that we are capable of much more. It's quite funny: there are many trainers at my gym, and most chit chat with their clients and explain exercises and count reps. Then there is one guy who really pushes his clients and gives them a hard time for not giving 100%. He actually gets in their face—although when he steps away has a smile on his face knowing it's part of the game. If I were to hire another trainer for myself, it would be a simple choice. He would get me to do my best.

3. Feedback and coaching

One of your problems is you have blind spots that you will likely never see. A good "advisor" will point out you these things whether you want to hear them or not. So it is not easy to find such people who will level with you. It's why you want your team to be people who can direct you where you want to go because they either have expertise in that area or can ask you the right questions and get enough leverage on yourself to take action.

Talking about your fears and obstacles is helpful so you become self-aware enough to do something differently. Committing to future action and to goals is the public declaration that I wrote about in the last chapter. It makes us more obligated to follow through.

Jugular dialogue: it's a time to talk about what matters most.

Jugular questions: What would do if you knew you couldn't fail?

4. Accountability

This helps you set higher goals and stretch your ideas of what's achievable. It's one reason why coaching works well. Is your non-coach partner tough enough to follow through consistently with this? Many people are not. Often peers get too close and no longer challenge each other. You will want to frequently remind each other that candid feedback is required.

There are advantages to hiring a coach because they've worked with many others in the same situation—that's their expertise. It's what they do every day. When it comes to referrals, if I am your coach, I know which direction to go.

There are advantages to having a peer-to-peer advisor: powerful emotional encouragement because your relationship has more depth.

Or have both! Have a coach for one area and a peer for another. Your team can help you put leverage on yourself to behave your way to what you want.

Who makes a good team advisor?

Besides a coach with a *proven track record*, think about those people you know who already read business books or invest in attending seminars. This means they already recognize the value of personal and professional development. Perhaps they are regulars in your trade or professional association. In your company it could be your manager or a top performer. Either way they are people who clearly want more from life and are willing to do something about it.

Your biggest challenge.

How you see the world is what determines the actions you take in every area of your life. Any self-respecting personal development book will tell you this. Stephen Covey calls them paradigms. Zaffron and Logan's first law of performance is: *"How people perform correlates to how situations occur to them."* Wayne Dyer explains that when you change the way you look at the world, the world you look at changes.

In other words, If you believe that getting referrals will always be tough for you, guess what—it will be! On the other hand, if you believe getting referrals is something you can do effectively from now on, you get results from this book.

Warning! Finding the right people for your advisor team is not easy! But, as you already know, neither is getting more referrals and reaching your dreams. Pretty much everyone can be bigger in life by finding the courage, guidance, support, and accountability that's often missing. Seek these people out and reap the rewards. I would be happy to be the referral coach for you.

Whatever you decide to do next, Take lots of action, persist, revisit what is in this book and have faith in yourself to know that, with a little bit of help and quite a bit of practice, you can get the results you want and deserve. I commend you for having taken this powerful step. By finishing this book you (really!) have put yourself in a tiny percentage of dedicated professionals. Now it's time to prove that you can fulfill your potential on this one journey on earth.

Bibliography.

Abraham, Richard. *Mr. Schmooze.* Richard Abraham Company

Alba, Jason. *I'm on LinkedIn: Now what???* Lincoln Valley: Happy About, 2007.

Allen, Robert G.. *Multiple Streams of Income.* NY: Wiley, 2000.

Armstrong, Lance, Sally Jenkins, *It's Not About the Bike.* NY: GP Putnam and Son, 2000

Arbinger Institute. *Leadership and Self-Deception.* San Francisco CA: Berrett-Koehler, 2000.

Bray- Attwood, Janet and Chris Attwood. *The Passion Test.* UK: Simon and Schuster, 2007.

Bach, David. *The Automatic Millionaire.* Broadway, 2005

Bachrach, Bill. *Values Based Selling.* San Diego CA: Aim High Publishing, 1996.

Baker, Dan. *What Happy People Know.* Rodale Inc., 2003.

Bannatyne, Duncan. *Anyone Can Do It.* London, UK: Orion books, 2006.

Beckwith, Harry and Christine Clifford- Beckwith. *You, Inc.* NY: Warner Business Books, 2007.

Beckwith, Harry. *Selling the Invisible.* NY: Time Warner Books, 1997.

Branden, Nathaniel. *The Six Pillars of Self-Esteem.* NY: Bantam, 1994.

Branden, Nathaniel. *How to Raise Your Self-Esteem.* NY: Bantam, 1987.

Branson, Richard. *Losing my Virginity.* NY: Three Rivers Press, 1999.

Branson, Richard. *Screw It, Let's Do It.* UK: Virgin Books, 2006.

Branson, Richard. *Business Stripped Bare.* London: Virgin Books, 2008.

Bridge, Rachel. *How I Made It.* London: Kogan-Page, 2005.

Brown, Gordon. *Courage.* NY: Weinstein, 2008.

Brown, Stuart. *Play.* London: Penguin, 2009.

Buckingham, Marcus and Donald Clifton. *Now, Discover Your Strengths.* NY: Free Press, 2001.

Buckingham, Marcus. *Go Put Your Strengths to Work.* NY: Free Press, 2007.

Burg, Bob. *Endless Referrals.* NY: McGraw-Hill, 1999.

Buscaglia, Leo. *Love.* NY: Vallentine Books, 1972.

Buscaglia, *Leo. Living, Loving and Learning.* Thoroughfare, NJ 1982.

Camp, Jim. *Start With No.* NY: Crown Business, 2002.

Canfield, Jack. *How to Have High Self Esteem.* Audio

Canfield, Jack. *The Success Principles.* NY: Harper Collins, 2005.

Canfield, Jack and Mark Victor Hansen. *The Aladdin Factor.* Audio

Carnegie, Dale. *How to Stop Worrying and Start Living.* NY: Simon and Schuster, 1984.

Carnegie, Dale. *How to Win Friends and Influence People.* NY: Simon and Schuster, 1982.

Cates, Bill. *Unlimited Referrals.* Silver Springs, Maryland: Thunder Hill Press, 1996.

Cates, Bill. *Get More Referrals Now!* NY: McGraw-Hill, 2004.

Chopra, Deepak. *Seven Spiritual Laws of Success.* San Rafael, CA: Amber-Allen Publishing,1994.

Cialdini, Robert B. *Influence: The Psychology of Persuasion.* NY: Harper-Collins, 2007.

Cialdini, Robert B., Noah J. Goldstein and Steve J. Martin. *Yes! 50 Secrets of Persuasion.* London UK: Profile Books, 2007.

Clason, George S. *The Richest Man in Babylon.* NY: Signet, 1988.

Collins, Jim. *Good to Great*. NY: Harper-Collins, 2001.

Colvin, Geoff. *Talent is Overrated.* NY: Portfolio, 2008.

Covey, Stephen R. *The 8th Habit.* NY: Free Press, 2004.

Covey, Stephen R. *The 7 Habits of Highly Effective People.* NY: Simon and Schuster, 1990.

Covey, Stephen R., Roger A. Merrill and Rebecca R. Merrill. *First Things First.* NY: Simon and Schuster, 1995.

Croner, Christopher and Richard Abraham. *Never Hire a Bad Sales Person Again.* Richard Abraham Company, 2006.

Csikszentmihalyi, Mihaly. *Flow: The Psychology of Optimal Experience.* NY: Harper and Row, 1990.

De Angles, Barbara. *Confidence.* Audio program.

Darling, Diane. *The Networking Survival Guide.* NY: McGraw-Hill, 2003.

Dragon's Den. *Success from Pitch to Profit.* London, UK: Harper Collins, 2007.

Dudley, George W. and Shannon L.Goodman. *The Psychology of Sales Call Reluctance.* Dallas, Texas: Behavioral Sciences Research Press, 1999.

Dyer, Wayne W.. *The Awakened Life.* Audio. Nightingale Conant.

Dyer, Wayne W.. *Wisdom of the Ages.* NY: Harper-Collins, 1998.

Dyer, Wayne W.. *The Power of Intention.* Carlsbad, CA: Hay House, 2004.

Dyer, Wayne W.. *You Will See It When You Believe It.* NY: Quill Press, 1989.

Easterbrook, Greg. *The Progress Paradox.* NY: Random House, 2004.

Eker, T. Harv. *Secrets of the Millionaire Mind.* NY: Harper Business, 2005.

Eliot, John. *Overachievement.* NY: Portfolio, 2004.

Eliot, John. *The Maverick Mindset.* Audio. Nightingale Conant.

Farber, Mary. *12 Clichés of Selling and Why They Work.* NY: Workman Publishing, 2001.

Ferrazzi, Keith. *Never Eat Alone.* NY: Currency, 2005.

Ferrazzi, Keith. *Who's Got Your Back.* NY: Broadway, 2009.

Ferriss, Timothy. *The 4-Hour Work Week.* NY: Crown, 2007.

Fisher, Donna. *Professional Networking for Dummies.* NY: Wiley, 2001.

Fisher, Donna and Andy Bilas. *Power Networking.* Marietta Georgia: Bard Press, 2000.

Fox, Michael J, *Always Looking Up.* NY: Hyperion, 2009

Fox, Jeffrey J. *How to Become a Rainmaker.* NY: Hyperion, 2000.

Frankl, Vicktor. *Man's Search for Meaning.* NY: Touchstone Books, 1984.

Gage, Randy. *Why You're Dumb, Sick and Broke…* Hoboken, NJ: Wiley, 2006.

Gallup Management Journal, various issues from 2006-2007.

Garrison, Steve. *The Five Secrets From Oz.* Booksurge Press, Charleston, SC. 2009

Gawain, Shakti. *Creative Visualization.* NY: Bantam, 1985.

Geghard, Nathan and Mike Marriner and Joanne Gordon. *Roadtrip Nation.* NY: Vallentine Books, 2003.

Gerber, Michael E. *The E-myth Revisited.* NY: Harper Business, 1995.

Gilbert, Daniel. *Stumbling on Happiness.* NY: Alfred A. Knopf, 2006.

Gitomer, Jeffery. *Little Red Book of Selling.* Austin, TX: Bard Press, 2005.

Gitomer, Jeffery. *Little Green Book of Getting Your Way.* Upper Saddle River NJ: FT Press, 2007.

Gitomer, Jeffery. *Little Platinum Book of Cha-Ching.* Upper Saddle River NJ: FT Press, 2007.

Gladwell, Malcom. *Outliers.* NY: Little, Brown and Company, 2008.

Gladwell, Malcom. *Blink.* Back Bay Books, 2007.

Gladwell, Malcom. *The Tipping Point.* Back Bay Books, 2002.

Godin, Seth. *Permission Marketing.* NY: Simon & Schuster, 1999.

Goldsmith, Marshall. *What Got You Here, Won't Get You There.* Audio. Random House, 2007.

Hallowell, Edward. *CrazyBusy.* Audio. Random House, 2006.

Harrold, Fiona. *Be Your Own Life Coach.* London: Coronet, 2001.

Harrold, Fiona. *The 10-Minute Life Coach.* London: Hodder and Stoughton, 2002.

Harrold, Fiona. *The 7 Rules of Success.* London: Hodder and Stoughton, 2006.

Holden, Robert. *Success Intelligence.* London: Hodder and Stoughton, 2005.

Hicks, Esther and Jerry Hicks. *Ask and It Is Given.* Carlsbad, CA: Hay House, 2004.

Hicks, Esther and Jerry Hicks. *Abraham's Greatest Hits.* Carlsbad, CA: Hay House, audio.

Hill, Napoleon. *Think and Grow Rich.* NY: Random House, 1988.

Hill, Napoleon. *Napoleon Hill's A Year of Growing Rich.* NY: Penguin, 1993.

Horsesmouth.com. *Automatic Referrals*. NY: Horsesmouth.com, 2005.

Investor's Business Daily. *Business Leaders and Success.* NY: McGraw-Hill, 2004.

Johnson, Cameron. *You Call the Shots*. NY: Free Press, 2007.

Johnson, Spencer. *The Present*. NY: Double Day, 2003.

Johnson, Spencer. *The One Minute Sales Person*. NY: Avon, 1986.

Koegel, Timothy J. *The Exceptional Presenter.* Austin, TX: Green Leaf, 2007.

Korsgaden, Troy. *Power Position your Agency*. Troy Korsgaden, 1998.

Lama, Dalai and Howard Cutler. *The Art of Happiness*. London: Hodder and Stoughton, 1998.

Lencioni, Patrick. *The Five Dysfunctions of a Team.* San Francisco CA: Josey-Bass, 2002.

Lester, David. *How They Started.* Richmond UK: Crimson, 2008.

Li, Charlene and Josh Bernoff. *Groundswell.* Boston Massachusetts: Forrester Research, 2008.

Lipton, Bruce. *The Biology of Belief*. Carlsbad, CA. Hay House. 2005.

Luntz, Frank. *Words that Work*. NY: Hyperion, 2007.

Mackay, Harvey. *Dig Your Well Before You're Thirsty*. NY: Currency,1999.

Mackay, Harvey. *How to Build a Network of Power Relationships*. NY: Simon & Schuster Audio, 1995.

Mandino, Og. *The Greatest Salesman in the World.* NY: Bantam, 1968.

Maxwell, John. *Thinking for a Change*. NY: Time Warner Books, 2003.

Maxwell, John. *The 21 Irrefutable Laws of Leadership.* Nashville, TN: Nelson, 1998.

Misner, Ivan and Don Morgan. *Masters of Success.* Entrepreneur Press, 2004.

Montoya, Peter. *The Brand Called You.* Audio. Nightingale Conant.

Morgenstern, Julie. *Organizing From the Inside Out*. NY: Henry Holt,1998.

Morgenstern, Julie. *Time Management from the Inside Out.* NY: Henry Holt, 2000.

Mullen, David J.. *The Million Dollar Financial Services Practice.* NY: AMA, 2008.

Naisbitt, John. *Megatrends.* NY: Warner Books, 1984.

Penn, Mark J. *Microtrends.* Audio. Hachette.

Peters, Tom. *The Circle of Innovation.* NY: Alfred A. Knopf, 1997.

Pine, B. Joseph and James H. Gilmore. *The Experience Economy.* Boston Massachusetts: HBS Press,1999.

Port, Michael. *Book Yourself Solid.* NY: John Wiley Hoboken, 2006.

Prince, Russ Alan and Lewis Schiff. *The Middle-Class Millionaire.* NY: Currency, 2008.

Rath, Tom and Donald O.Clifton. *How Full is Your Bucket?* NY: Gallup Press, 2004.

Reynolds, Garr. *Presentation Zen.* Berkeley, CA: New Writers, 2008.

Richardson, Cheryl. *Take Time for Your Life.* NY: Broadway Books, 1999.

Reis, Al and Jack Trout. *22 Immutable Laws of Marketing*. NY: Harper Business, 1993.

Robbins, Anthony. *Awaken the Giant Within.* NY: Simon & Schuster, 1992.

Robbins, Anthony. *Personal Power!* Robbins Research International, 1989.

Robbins, Anthony. *The Power to Shape Your Destiny.* Audio. Nightingale Conant.

Robbins, Anthony. *Unlimited Power.* NY: Free Press, 1997.

Rock, David. *Personal Best.* Sydney: Simon and Schuster, 2001

Roddick, Anita. *Body and Soul.* Vermilion, 1992.

Sanborn, Mark. *The Fred Factor.* NY: Currency, 2004.

Sanders, Tim. *Love Is The Killer App.* NY: Three Rivers Press, 2003.

Sanders, Tim. *The Likeability Factor.* NY: Crown Publisher, 2005.

Sandler Sales Institute, *Closing the Sale,* Nightingale Conant audio program.

Sernovitz, Andy. *Word of Mouth Marketing.* NY: Kaplan, 2006.

Sharma, Robin. *Who Will Cry When You Die?* Carlsbad, CA: Hay House, 2002.

Shapiro, Stephen M.. *Goal Free Living.* Hoboken, NJ: Wiley, 2006.

Sheahan, Peter. *Generation Y.* Victoria Australia: HGB, 2006.

Sher, Barbara and Anne Gottlieb. *Wishcraft.* NY: Vallentine Books, 1979.

Sher, Barbara and Barbara Smith. *I Could Do Anything If I Only Knew What it Was.* NY: DTP, 1994.

Smith, Benson and Tony Rutigliano. *Discover Your Sales Strengths.* Warner, 2003.

Souza, Brian, *Become Who You Were Born to Be.* NY, Harmony, 2005.

Stanley, Thomas J. *The Millionaire Mind.* Kansas City: Andrews McNeil, 2001.

Stanley, Thomas J. *Networking with Millionaires... and Their Advisors.* NY: Simon & Schuster Audio, 2001

Stanley, Thomas J, *Marketing to the Affluent.*NY: McGraw Hill, 1997.

Stanley, Thomas J. and William Danko. *The Millionaire Next Door.* NY: Simon & Schuster, 1999.

Stoltz, Paul G. and Erik Weihenmayer. *The Adversity Advantage.* NY: Fireside, 2006.

Stone, Rosamund and Benjamin Zander. *The Art of Possibility.* NY: Penguin Books, 2000.

Switzer, Janet. *Instant Income.* NY: McGraw-Hill, 2007.

Tancer, Bill. *Click.* London, UK: Harper Collins, 2009.

Templar, Richard. *The Rules of Life.* Harlow UK: Pearson, 2006.

Templeton, Tim. *The Referral of a Lifetime.* San Francisco CA: BK Publishers, 2004.

Thaler, Richard H. and Cass R Sunstein. *Nudge.* New Haven: Yale University Press, 2008.

Thomson, Peter. *The Best-Kept Secrets of the World's Great Achievers.* Audio. Nightingale Conant.

Tracy, Brian. *Accelerated Learning Techniques.* Audio. Nightingale Conant.

Tracy, Brian. *Advanced Selling Techniques.* Audio. Nightingale Conant.

Tracy, Brian. *Goals!* San Francisco, CA: BK Publishers, 2003.

Tracy, Brian. *Change Your Thinking Change Your Life.* Hoboken, NJ: Wiley, 2003.

Tracy, Brian. *Maximum Achievement.* NY: Fireside, 1995.

Tracy, Brian. *Many Miles To Go.* Irvine CA: Entrepreneur Press, 2003.

Tracy, Brian. *The Power of Clarity*. Audio. Nightingale Conant.

Tracy, Brian. *The Psychology of Selling*. Audio. Nightingale Conant.

Tracy, Brian. *The Science of Self Confidence.* Audio. Nightingale Conant.

Welch, Jack and Suzy Welch. *Winning.* NY: Harper Business, 2005.

West, Scott and Mitch Antony. *Storyselling for Financial Advisors.* Chicago: Dearborn, 2000.

Whitmore, John. *Coaching for Performance*. London: NB, 1996.

Wooden, John and Steve Jamison. *The Essential Wooden.* NY: McGraw-Hill, 2007.

Zaffron, Steve and Dave Logan. *The 3 Laws of Performance.* San Francisco CA: Josey-Bass, 2009.

Ziglar, Zig. *Success and the Self-Image.* Audio. Nightingale Conant, 1995.

Ziglar, Zig. *The Secrets to Closing the Sale.* Audio

THE LOYALTY EZINE:

The Client Loyalty Top-of-Mind Marketing Program.

Instead of sending your contacts industry-related content that they never read, be the one sending them words of inspiration and a message of hope.

What is The *Loyalty E-Zine*?

It is a monthly e-newsletter that revitalizes your marketing by bringing **useful and inspiring information** to your database: your prospects and your past and present clients. **It adds real value.**

Why is The *Loyalty E-Zine* Such an Efficient, Innovative and Simple Investment in Your Business?

There are two versions available: The Hassle-free Version OR **The Word Document Version**

Hassle Free Version: Offers Easy, turn-key approach that requires no work on your part! (After initial set up.)

Or would you like to write your own E-Zine every month? Our **Word Document Version** will supply you with two articles every month to get you started and then it's up to you to take care of the rest.

You will receive Measurable Results because you will **GET MORE REFERRALS!**

Testimonials from our latest recipients of the Loyalty E-Zine!!!

"I like this! I just skimmed it and decided to print it out and read it on the bus ride in to work. Should help the day start much better! Keep me on your list!"

"I enjoyed the email and will send it to others. Very thought provoking."

Imagine the Benefits to This Hassle-Free Investment!

1. **A one-time payment of only $495 for 12 months plus a $99 activation fee: SAVE almost $100!**

2. **Completely Hassle-Free Version: Only $49/month for a 12 month subscription plus $99 activation fee!**
3. **The Word Document Version: $24.95/month for a 12 month subscription.**

Call (608) 843-3827 or email contact@TheReferralAuthority.com
SIGN UP NOW! www.LoyaltyEzine.com

Index

Made in the USA
Charleston, SC
14 March 2010